HISTORIC SCOTLAND

PREHISTORIC ORKNEY

ANNA RITCHIE

B. T. Batsford Ltd/Historic Scotland
London

For my husband, Graham, who introduced me to Orkney

First published 1995
Reprinted 1997

Typeset by Servis Filmsetting Ltd
and printed in Great Britain by
The Bath Press, Bath

Published by B. T. Batsford Ltd
583 Fulham Road, London SW6 5BY

A CIP catalogue record for this book is available from the British Library

ISBN 0 7134 7593 5 (limp)

Contents

Illustrations

Colour plates

Acknowledgements

Over the years I have benefited from discussions with many colleagues working in Orkney, and I am grateful to them for their contribution to this book. In particular, I should like to thank Caroline Wickham-Jones for information about Mesolithic Orkney, John Barber for information about Sand Fiold and John Hedges for his thought-provoking work on Orkney and for the map of brochs on which the map here (73) is based. I am especially grateful to Audrey Henshall, Anne Brundle, Patrick Ashmore and Noel Fojut for their kindness in reading and commenting on chapters, and to David Breeze and Graham Ritchie for reading the whole book to great effect. My father-in-law, W.F. Ritchie, has become indispensable as my linguistic mentor, and I am deeply indebted to him. I have greatly appreciated the help and encouragement provided by Peter Kemmis Betty and Charlotte Kilenyi of Batsford.

David Henrie of Historic Scotland was kind enough to take superb photographs specially for this volume, and Alan Braby created the reconstruction drawings with his customary flair, as well as drawing (except 68) most of the other line illustrations. I am very grateful to them both, and to Gunnie Moberg who allowed me to use one of her evocative photographs of land and sea (1).

I am indebted to the following individuals and institutions for photographs, for which they own the copyright: Lord Renfrew of Kaimsthorn (71), Raymond Lamb (95), Graham Ritchie (27–8, colour plate 1), Archaeological Operations and Conservation Scotland (68), Crown Copyright: Royal Commission on the Ancient and Historical Monuments of Scotland (3, 24, 26, 38–9, 41, 45, 57–9, 64, 72, 84, 91–2), The Orkney Library, Photographic Archive (83), Trustees of the National Museums of Scotland (51–4, 69, colour plate 7, back cover), Ingval Maxwell (colour plate 5). All the remaining illustrations are Crown Copyright: Historic Scotland.

Introduction

Orkney is an archaeologist's paradise. The islands have always been attractive to human settlement and an unusual amount of evidence for life in ancient times has survived in the form of upstanding monuments. There are several factors that have ensured their preservation, as we shall see, such as the effect of good building stone and the Orcadian pride in the past; the net result has been an astounding heritage of ancient monuments which illuminate social development throughout prehistory. For the purposes of this book, prehistory covers some four thousand years from the earliest evidence of a human presence in the fourth millennium BC to the dawn of history in the middle centuries of the first millennium AD. Overall, the chapters that follow are arranged chronologically, but the two thousand years from about 4000 to about 2000 BC have left such a richness of material that they are treated thematically, according to the evidence for domestic life, for the traditions surrounding death, for art and ceremony and social organization.

Attracted by the wealth of visible monuments, antiquaries and latterly archaeologists have been drawn to Orkney (1) to swell the efforts of local scholars, and Orcadian excavations have figured large in the study of past societies, which has expanded rapidly since the mid-nineteenth century (2).

The first Ancient Monuments Act was passed by Parliament in 1882, although it had taken almost ten years from its introduction owing to opposition from landowners who feared that their interests were at risk. Part of the Act was a Schedule of Monuments considered worthy of preservation, and in this Maes Howe, the Ring of Brodgar and the Stones of Stenness in Orkney were included. Other Acts concerned with ancient monuments have been passed since then, and the Schedule has expanded enormously; some of the most important monuments were gradually taken into the direct care of the State. Orkney's heritage fared particularly well, with a total of 35 prehistoric and historic sites in guardianship by 1975. The first Inspector of Ancient Monuments was one of the great archaeologists of the last century, Lieutenant-General Augustus Henry Lane Fox Pitt Rivers, and his tours of inspection included a number of visits to Scotland in the 1880s, and to Orkney in particular in 1885. There was less threat to Orcadian monuments than to many elsewhere, however, and two decades passed before the first were taken into care in 1906, namely the two great stone circles known as the Ring of Brodgar and the Stones of Stenness. The monuments in State care in Orkney range now from tombs and houses built more than 5000 years ago to a corn-mill and a defensive tower of nineteenth-century date.

In 1908, a Royal Commission on the Ancient and Historical Monuments of Scotland was set up to record all the monuments older than 1707 surviving in Scotland (1707 being the date of the Act of Union between Scotland and England),

and to recommend those most worthy of preservation. The three volumes of the *Inventory of the Ancient Monuments of Orkney and Shetland* were published in 1946; the fieldwork had been carried out in the late 1920s and 1930s, but war intervened and publication had to be deferred. These volumes are still invaluable as a source of information, and this is reflected by their price in the antiquarian book market! The Commission's work in Orkney coincided with a vigorous period of excavation, and its officers were sometimes involved in recording newly dug monuments, such as Knap of Howar in Papa Westray, which Charles Calder surveyed. When this early farm was re-excavated in the 1970s, a piece of archaeological history was found. At the very spot where Calder's plane table had stood while he was planning the houses in 1934 was discovered his rubber!

Orkney Islands Council is now closely involved in caring for the built heritage. Amongst other projects have been the restoration of a beehive-shaped dovecot of seventeenth-century date at Hall of Rendall, northeast of Finstown, and the consolidation and roofing of a chambered tomb at Isbister in South Ronaldsay. Tourism in the islands has been boosted by informative leaflets and heritage trails, and the natural environment and ancient monuments are seen to be equal aspects of Orkney's past, present and future. Appropriately, North Sea oil refined in the island of Flotta helped to fund, through the Orkney Heritage Society, the establishment in the 1970s of the post of Orkney Archaeologist, who created a Sites and Monuments Record for Orkney and thus began to update the Royal Commission *Inventory*. The Orkney Archaeologist and the Museums Officer at Tankerness House Museum in Kirkwall are the people to whom any archaeological discovery should be reported, whether it is an object or a site.

1 *Seascape at Yesnaby: the west coast of Orkney faces the Atlantic waves (Gunnie Moberg).*

Orcadian antiquaries

Far too many monuments were unscientifically dug and poorly recorded in the nineteenth century, but some useful work was done. Two figures in particular dominate the middle decades of the century, a local factor and Sheriff Clerk, George Petrie, and a frequent summer visitor to the islands, James Farrer, Member of Parliament for Durham South. Petrie was by far the better antiquary and he recorded the excavations of others as well as his own, thus rendering a considerable service to Orcadian archaeology. Although his records were not all published, the manuscripts were preserved by the Society of Antiquaries of Scotland and can be consulted today in the library of the National Museums of Scotland and in the National Monuments Record of Scotland in Edinburgh. Among his excavations were a major Iron Age settlement at Lingro (p.106) and several Neolithic chambered tombs, one of which, in the Holm of Papa Westray, was re-excavated in the 1980s (p.41).

James Farrer's most famous exploit was opening the great mound of Maes Howe, a familiar landmark beside the road between Stromness and Finstown (p.55). One Saturday afternoon in July 1861, encouraged by the news that 'several gentlemen of well-known antiquarian reputation from Edinburgh and Aberdeen' were expected to arrive in Orkney on the *Prince Consort* steamship, Farrer set his workmen on to digging into the side of the mound. Work resumed on the Monday, and they broke through the roof of the entrance passage; discovering it to be full of earth and stones, Farrer decided to take a quicker route through the top of the mound, and, 'after a few day's labour the whole of the rubbish filling the chamber was removed'. He and his visitors were delighted to find that the walls of the well-preserved chamber bore a large number of inscriptions carved in the old Norse runic alphabet, the first to be found in Orkney and even now the largest surviving collection of runes on stone. They showed that Farrer and his men were not the first to break

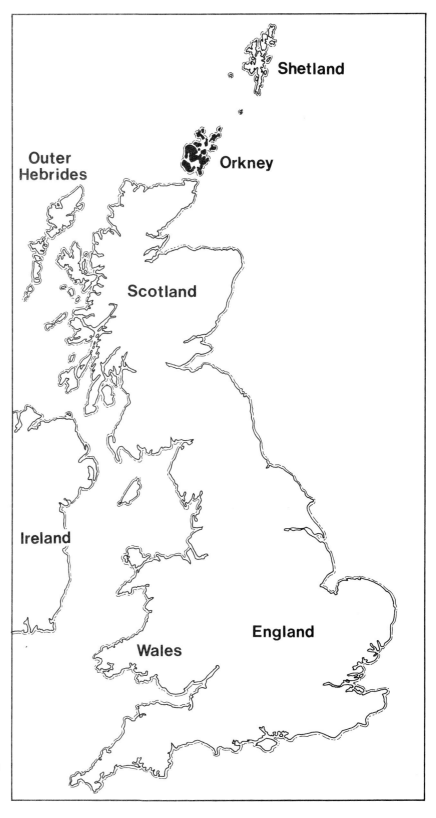

2 *Map showing the location of Orkney in the British Isles.*

into Maes Howe, for Norsemen had beaten them to it six centuries earlier. Immense care was taken in recording the runic inscriptions, for not only were they drawn by George Petrie, but two sets of casts were made for museums in Edinburgh and Copenhagen. A monograph entitled *Notice of Runic Inscriptions discovered during recent excavations in the Orkneys* was printed for private circulation in Edinburgh in 1862; bound in green leather embossed in gold, it contains two beautiful colour lithographs, one of which is reproduced here in black and white (**3**).

The 1920s and 1930s were full of antiquarian action in Orkney. The work of local scholars was published both nationally in the *Proceedings of the Society of Antiquaries of Scotland* and in the *Proceedings* of their own Orkney Antiquarian Society, which had been founded in 1922. In the roll-call of the Society of Antiquaries of Scotland for 1930, no fewer than ten Orcadians are listed as Fellows. They range from the landowner on Papa Westray, William Traill, elected Fellow in 1917, to an architect, Thomas Peace, elected in 1891, a Master Mariner on Westray, John Craigie, elected in 1928, and the Manager of the Orkney Steam Navigation Company, Donald Bertram, elected in 1929. Many more were members of the Orkney Antiquarian Society, and they studied place-names, genealogy and folklore as well as history and archaeology. There was a long tradition of awareness and pride in Orkney's past, and it was a courageous, or foolhardy, farmer who risked damaging any part of the ancient heritage. A famous incident happened in December 1814. A tenant farmer in Stenness, not himself an Orcadian, broke up a standing stone known as the Stone of Odin and began to destroy the nearby stone circle, the Stones of Stenness. There was such a public outcry that an action was threatened in the Sheriff Court to restrain him from any more damage. In the event he apologized and promised to 'desist from his operations'.

Typical of the good work carried out by the Orkney Antiquarian Society was its prompt reaction to the discovery of an earth-house at the farm of Rennibister in Mainland (p.116). One Friday morning in November 1926, a

3 *Maes Howe in 1861 before Farrer's excavation; in the distance are the Stones of Stenness, the Watchstone and the Ring of Brodgar.*

4 *Professor V. Gordon Childe at Skara Brae in 1929.*

steam-thresher was coming out of the stackyard gate when the ground gave way beneath its wheels and it became stuck in a large hole; it was hauled out of the hole which proved to be an underground chamber. That afternoon, three members of the Society went out to inspect the chamber and pronounced it to be an earth-house, and the following day the Secretary, Dr Hugh Marwick, went out there with two work-men to excavate it, recording the work in the Society's *Proceedings*.

One monument above all others had an enormous impact on local interest, and proved to be the spur to other excavations. Professor V. Gordon Childe, the first holder of the Aber-cromby Chair of Archaeology in the University of Edinburgh, had been brought in by the Office of Works in 1928 to supervise the work at Skara Brae, which was being revealed as an astound-ingly well-preserved prehistoric village (4). Fired by this demonstration of what could lie hid-den beneath Orcadian turf, William Traill of

Holland in Papa Westray and his friend William Kirkness embarked in 1929 upon the excavation of Knap of Howar, another example of prehis-toric houses preserved virtually to roof-level, and Walter G. Grant in the same year began a productive series of excavations in Rousay (5). That summer also saw the initial exploration of the great mound covering the broch of Gurness by Robert Rendall, best known for his poetry but drawn to the practical side of archaeology and a member of the Orkney Antiquarian Society. The Society lapsed at the outbreak of the Second World War, but its history and achievements were later charted by Robert Rendall and published in *The Orcadian* newspaper in 1967. It was clearly a lively as well as learned Society: 'There was a sort of inner cabinet composed of acknowledged "experts", but also a sturdy row of "backbenchers" who noted every move and were ready, when it was fitting to do so, to intervene during "question-time" with observations.'

Orcadian archaeology has benefited, as every-where else has, from the development of scien-tific methods of dating, although many more series of accurate dates are still needed to amplify and underpin the basic chronology. The tech-nique of dating by radiocarbon analysis has played the greatest role; this depends upon the fact that all living organisms absorb radioactive carbon from the atmosphere and, after death, that carbon begins to decay at a known rate. By measuring the amount of radioactive carbon remaining in a sample, the age of death can be estimated, usually to within two hundred years. These are, however, radiocarbon years, and the real calendar date must be calculated by compar-ison with dates from tree-rings (known as dendrochronology); each growing season produces a distinct and visible ring in the horizontal section of a tree, and these rings can be counted and overlapping series can be built up from a number of trees. Combined with a test-series of radiocarbon dates from the same wood, a standard graph can be constructed and used to transform other radiocarbon dates into calendar dates. Calendar dates obtained in this way will be used throughout this book.

Overall the aim has been to use a framework of calendar dates, but sometimes it has been convenient to use the traditional blanket terms of the three-age system, which was devised in the nineteenth century and which still has some value today. The three ages were the Stone Age, the Bronze Age and the Iron Age, and they were subsequently broken down into earlier and later phases. In line with common practice, in this book the terms Mesolithic and Neolithic are used in preference to middle and late Stone Age to describe the hunter-gatherer and early farming communities who were the first inhabitants of Orkney. The Bronze Age and the Iron Age are still useful terms when more precise calendar

dates are lacking or when a general impression of date is all that is needed. There is a glossary at the end of the book to explain archaeological words.

There are many exciting archaeological remains to visit in Orkney, and particularly good interpretative displays may be seen in Tankerness House Museum in Kirkwall. Many Orcadian artefacts take pride of place in the National Museums of Scotland in Edinburgh as part of the story of Scotland through the long centuries of prehistory.

5 The broch of Midhowe is protected by a modern sea-wall, and beyond can be seen the 'hanger' enclosing the stalled cairn of Midhowe. The foreshore provided an endless supply of building slabs.

CHAPTER ONE

Orkney, land and sea

The islands of Orkney lie off the north-east tip of mainland Scotland, separated by the turbulent waters of the Pentland Firth. At its narrowest point, the Firth is only about 6 miles wide, but on a rough day the crossing even in modern boats can feel interminable. There are about 40 islands and many small islets and skerries in the archipelago, creating a coastline some 500 miles long, but only mainland and 17 other islands are currently inhabited. Some 374 square miles in extent, most of the land consists of Old Red Sandstone with a covering of boulder clay (6). An understanding of the geology of Orkney was established during the nineteenth century, and there was particular interest in the strata containing fossil fish, the Sandwick Fish Bed in west mainland Orkney and the fish beds of Rousay and Eday.

Much of Orkney has a gentle domesticated appearance, low-lying with smooth contours clothed by green pasture or peat sometimes disguised by a topping of heather (7). The hills have rounded profiles and none is high, though the hills of Hoy appear high in relation to the rest of the landscape; the summits in Hoy reach a maximum of only 479m (1571ft) on Ward Hill. The reason for this distinctive topography is that much of Orkney was literally drowned by rising seas after the last Ice Age, and the surviving islands are but the uppermost strata of a landscape that might have existed had the effects of the melting ice behaved differently. As the map shows (8), a drop in today's sea-level of 10

fathoms would join most of the islands into three large islands, with the barest gap between Eday and Sanday/Stronsay. In fact, although the drowning process is still operating very slowly, there is likely to have been a difference of sea-level of only a few metres over the last six or seven millennia, the period during which Orkney has been inhabited by people. The major factor affecting the Orkney coastline today, as ever, is erosion; a bad winter storm can break away several metres of exposed cliff-face. Erosion, combined with even a small rise in sea-level, has considerable archaeological implications; not only have many sites been lost into the sea, but some small islands were probably promontories in early times. The chambered tombs on the Holm of Papa Westray, for example, give a fine impression of an island of the dead, but, at the time when they were built and used, the Holm was almost certainly a promontory on the east coast of Papa Westray (see pp.41–4).

Despite its gentle landscape, there are plenty of dramatic visual contrasts in Orkney. The east coasts of Sanday and North Ronaldsay rise so imperceptibly from the sea that in storm conditions the islands are invisible to sailors; one of the four earliest lighthouses to be built in Scotland was on Dennis Head, North Ronaldsay, constructed in AD 1789, and another on Start Point, Sanday, soon followed in the early years of the nineteenth century. In contrast, many of the western and northern stretches of coastline, particularly in Hoy, Mainland, Rousay and

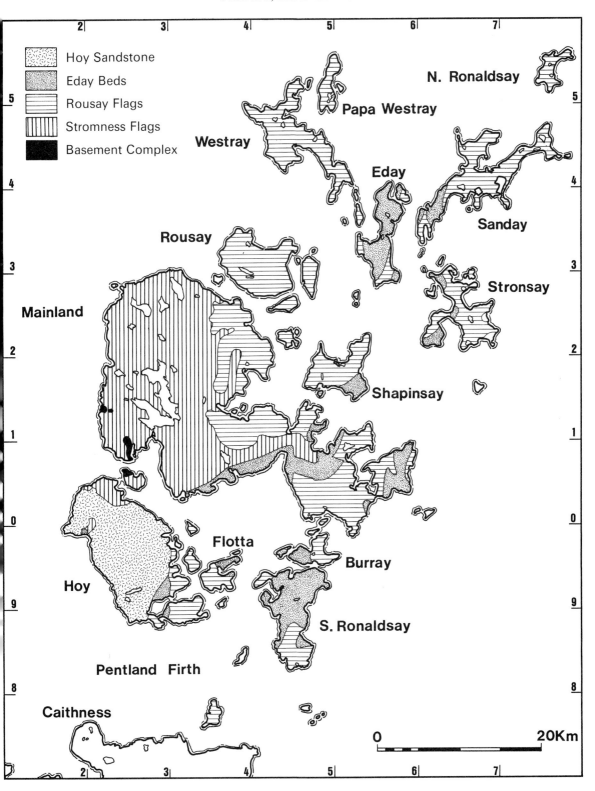

Hoy Sandstone
Eday Beds
Rousay Flags
Stromness Flags
Basement Complex

N. Ronaldsay

Papa Westray

Westray

Eday

Sanday

Rousay

Stronsay

Mainland

Shapinsay

Flotta

Burray

Hoy

S. Ronaldsay

Pentland Firth

Caithness

0   20Km

6 *Geological map of Orkney*

Westray, consist of awesome near-vertical cliffs hundreds of metres high – the highest in western Hoy rise some 300m (984ft) above the hammering Atlantic waves.

Natural resources

The most essential raw material which has contributed to the richness of the archaeological record in Orkney is building stone. The lower strata of the Old Red Sandstone include the beds known as the Stromness and Rousay flags; these produce grey flagstones which effectively dress themselves ready for building. The rock is bedded horizontally and it splits into flat even slabs with straight edges. These can be prised up easily, using wooden wedges which swell when wet, and on beaches such slabs lie detached and ready for use, ideal for walling, paving and roofs. A skilful quarryman could achieve any variety of thick or thin slab to suit the purpose, especially the large thin slabs used in prehistoric times for

8 (Opposite) *Map of Orkney showing land over 75m (246ft) OD, the 10-fathom submarine contour, lighthouses and sources of lead, copper and iron ore.*

room divisions and in recent times for roofing. The passage leading into the chamber at Maes Howe is lined on either side with slabs averaging 5.6m (18ft 3in) long, 1.2m (4ft) deep and 0.17m (7in) thick, which must have been carefully chosen and quarried (9).

Sandstone cobbles from the beach were used for a wide variety of tools such as hammers and anvils, and large flakes knocked off such cobbles became simple but remarkably versatile cutting tools. These are known as Skaill knives, because a large number was found at Skara Brae on the Bay of Skaill, but they are typical late Neolithic artefacts throughout Orkney and Shetland.

Other local rocks were used for tools, notably the intrusive dykes of igneous rock thrown up by volcanic action in geological times. Many of these dykes are of camptonite, which is suitable for polished stone axes and stone balls. Flint and chert were made into small items such as

7 *A typical landscape in eastern Mainland.*

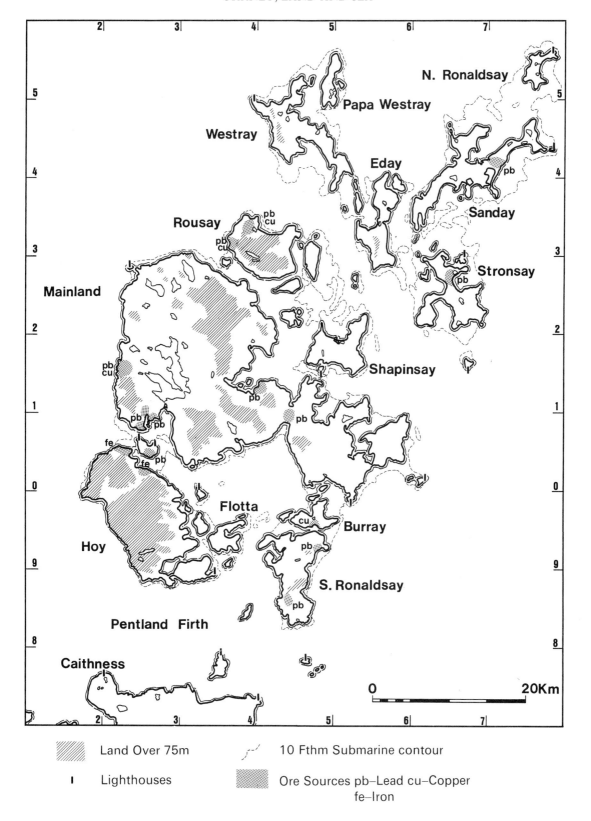

Land Over 75m

Lighthouses

10 Fthm Submarine contour

Ore Sources pb–Lead cu–Copper
fe–Iron

9 *The passage into the tomb at Maes Howe, showing one of the huge side-slabs, 5.6m (18.4ft) long.*

scrapers, arrowheads and knife blades, and both could be found locally, though only as relatively small nodules. Flint nodules occur in boulder clay deposits in the islands of Swona and Stroma in the Pentland Firth and in North Ronaldsay, but most flint is likely to have been gathered from the beaches, derived ultimately from deposits beneath the sea off the east coast of Scotland. Chert, which is a flint-like quartz, occurs as pebbles both in boulder clay in Shapinsay and in the Old Red Sandstone strata in Eday and western Mainland. Chert was normally used as a local substitute for flint, but the quality of beach flint is not high, and chert may sometimes have been a deliberate preference (see p.34).

Several minerals of interest to prehistoric peoples can be found in Orkney, but the problem lies in proving that they were exploited in early times. Ore deposits of lead, copper and silver are known in Mainland and six other islands, and haematite, an excellent iron ore, occurs in Hoy (see 8). Nodules of haematite with flat highly polished facets have been found at Skara Brae, suggesting that they had been used to produce a smooth glossy finish on leather.

Pumice derived from volcanic eruptions in Iceland was washed up on beaches and was commonly used throughout prehistoric times for shaping and sharpening the points of bone tools and dress pins.

Climate and vegetation

Despite its northerly latitude, Orkney has an equable climate with no extremes of temperature owing to the fact that the Gulf Stream passes close by. But it does suffer very high winds, and the wind factor has affected life in the islands from early times. Onshore wind speeds appear to have increased around 3800 BC, leading to loss of tall vegetation, showering of the land with salt-spray and movement of wind-blown sand. In some places the sand began to form dune-systems and in others lay as a thin layer over the land which improved its fertility.

Information derived from pollen analysis and from the remains of land-snails gives an impression of the vegetational cover in early times. There were birch, hazel and willow trees in the fourth millennium, but the increasing winds together with woodland clearance by the early colonists ensured that by 3000 BC these were reduced to little more than patches of scrub in open grassland.

The search for fuel must have presented an almost daily problem until the sustained and widespread growth of peat began in the later second millennium. Before then, the options were necessarily varied – and equally varied in their effectiveness. Apart from low scrub, which burned fast, homegrown wood was too precious to squander, and good driftwood was essential for building purposes. Dried seaweed, dried animal dung, turf, and bone could all become reasonable fuel to eke out timber supplies. Even in recent centuries, the inhabitants of the islands of Sanday and North Ronaldsay, where there was no peat, had to make do with seaweed, turf and dung. The latter would be dried cattle dung which gave a better light in the house than either seaweed or turf. Seaweed was at least an inexhaustible resource, whereas burning turf reduced the area of pasture, and cattle dung might have been used to better long-term purpose as an agricultural fertiliser. Excavations at Pool and Tofts Ness in Sanday revealed dumps of orange and red soil which have been interpreted as the result of burning peaty turf with a high iron content.

Despite an overall deterioration in the Orcadian climate that began around 3800 BC and has lasted to the present day, the climate in the later fourth millennium BC was slightly warmer than today, a difference of perhaps two degrees which was enough to make everyday life easier. The evidence for this climatic difference lies in discoveries of cereal grains and fish on archaeological sites. Wheat as well as barley was grown by the people of Skara Brae, whereas the farmers of recent times have not risked a wheat crop, preferring the hardier barley and oats. Many bones of the corkwing wrasse were found in the chambered tomb at Quanterness and red sea bream was found in the tomb at Midhowe; these are both fish which are rare in such northern latitudes today, and their presence indicates that the temperature of the sea must have been warmer in Neolithic times.

Animal and marine resources

Orkney was gradually separated from mainland Scotland by about 11,000 BC, by which time a number of small mammals had established themselves, including the Orkney vole, a sub-species unique to these islands whose bones have been found on archaeological sites. Thereafter, newcomers to the mammal population are most likely to have been introduced by human settlers, either deliberately or inadvertently. Even red deer, which swim well, are considered more likely to have been been transported along with other livestock, although, once in Orkney, they would have swum freely from island to island. Certainly the cattle, sheep and pigs reared by the earliest farmers had to be imported (10).

Orkney's greatest asset in terms of food resources was its long coastline and easy access to the sea. Fish, shellfish, seals and whales were abundant, and there was a choice of sheltered inshore fishing or the wide horizons of the Atlantic Ocean and the North Sea. It has always seemed likely to archaeologists that this good

10 *Artist's impression of the first farmers arriving in Orkney.*

fishing would have attracted groups of hunter-gatherers to Orkney, at least on a seasonal basis even if they were not living permanently in the islands, but their presence has been hard to prove. It depends upon finding flint tools of types which are known from elsewhere in Scotland to have been characteristic of the hunter-gatherers of the Mesolithic period, the period which preceded and overlapped with the Neolithic period of the earliest farming peoples. To make the search more difficult, flintwork that looks Mesolithic can turn up on Neolithic sites, such as Knap of Howar, where it is more likely to indicate the survival of old-fashioned ideas in tool-kits than pre-Neolithic activity. There may well have been intermarriage between the old population and the new colonists, and doubtless the new ideas of farming were adopted by people previously accustomed to living by hunting and fishing.

Recent fieldwork by Caroline Wickham-Jones at Millfield in Stronsay was designed to explore the place where a tanged flint point of apparently very early date had been found in the 1920s, in the hope of identifying a Mesolithic camp-site. Although more flint tools were found, and the presence of prehistoric activity confirmed, the flintwork was not sufficiently diagnostic to allow the site to be claimed as Mesolithic. A disappointing result, but one day proof of the presence in Orkney of hunter-gatherers may be found. They were certainly present in Caithness, and it seems unlikely that they failed to explore the islands so enticingly visible across the Pentland Firth.

When was Orkney colonized?

At present the earliest radiocarbon dates from Orkney come from the domestic settlement at Knap of Howar in Papa Westray, where they indicate occupation from about 3600 to about 3100 BC. But this is a fully fledged Neolithic farm and there must have been earlier and more experimental settlements belonging to pioneering times. These may have been more concerned with a pastoral economy based on cattle and sheep or goats than with agriculture (see **12**). The farming settlement of Shetland seems also to have been underway by the middle of the fourth millennium, to judge by the evidence from Scord of Brouster near Bridge of Walls. Not surprisingly, the first settlers in Orkney are likely to have come from Caithness, because the earliest chambered tombs in Orkney are closely related in design to those in Caithness. In Shetland, however, the design of houses and tombs appears to have become distinct from the start, despite the likelihood of the settlers having arrived via Orkney and Fair Isle. There is no evidence of direct contact with Scandinavia in either Shetland or Orkney – and by the early centuries of the third millennium Orkney's links were with the Western Isles and Ireland and with mainland Britain.

CHAPTER TWO

Everyday life

Erosion in the 1920s along the west coast of Papa Westray revealed rich deposits of midden material and walling at a hillocky patch of sand-dunes appropriately named Knap of Howar, which means 'mound of mounds'. The site lay on the lands of Holland, the major estate in Papa Westray, which was owned by William Traill. Robert Rendall described Traill as 'the friendly gadfly' of the Orkney Antiquarian Society, and he was clearly a very lively and provocative participant in the meetings in Kirkwall that he managed to attend. Inspired doubtless by the excavations at Skara Brae, Traill decided in 1929 to excavate his own prehistoric settlement with the help of his friend, William Kirkness. Not only was the partnership very successful, but it resulted in the earliest archaeological film made in Scotland, which Kirkness shot after the end of the excavation. His interest in photography also had the effect of making Knap of Howar an unusually well-recorded excavation in terms of black-and-white photographs.

A blanket of windblown sand 2.5m (8.2ft) thick had to be removed before the structures were revealed. These proved to be two stone-built houses, side by side and linked by a passage through their conjoining walls (**11**). They were well-preserved, with walls standing almost to full height in places and the lintel-slabs still in place over the doorways. A few artefacts were found, but nothing very helpful for dating purposes, and the houses were published as Iron Age in date, although privately William Traill believed them to be much older. The site was accepted into State care in 1937, and a sea-wall was built to protect the two houses. Robbed of their supportive blanket of sand, however, the walls began to deteriorate and eventually to collapse, and new excavations were undertaken in the 1970s by the writer on behalf of Historic Scotland to prepare the site for repair work. At the same time, it was hoped that dating evidence might be found, if not through new artefacts, at least through organic material which could be given radiocarbon analysis.

Traill's belief in the great age of the houses proved to be justified. Sherds were found of a very distinctive pottery, known as Unstan Ware, which was familiar from Neolithic chambered tombs in Orkney. It is characterized by round-bottomed bowls, which have a decorated collar above an angled shoulder. A Neolithic date was then confirmed by a series of radiocarbon analyses of animal bones, which gave a timespan of some 500 years, from about 3600 BC to about 3100 BC. Despite its location on one of the most northerly islands, Knap of Howar is among the earliest domestic settlements known in Scotland.

As always on domestic sites, most of the information about the lifestyle of the inhabitants came from their rubbish. The two houses were flanked on either side by midden, up to half a metre (1ft 8in) thick, which contained bones of animals, birds and fish, marine shells and the shells of tiny land-snails, along with broken pottery and discarded artefacts. Unfortunately,

11 *The two houses at Knap of Howar on the west coast of Papa Westray.*

soil conditions were not favourable to the preservation of pollen, but the land-snails provided a clear picture of the contemporary environment. Different types of land-snails prefer certain types of habitat, and these particular snails indicate that the settlement lay in open grassland well back from the seashore, probably protected from the sea by sand-dunes, and that there were freshwater pools in the vicinity. Before the site was established, there had been light woodland in the area, and the change to a more open habitat can probably be attributed to a combination of natural and human interference. Charcoal from the floor deposit in one of the houses proved to be driftwood, either spruce or larch, while charcoal from the midden represented native alder and birch. Remains of shellfish added more information about the nearby coast, because they included large numbers of oyster shells; oysters breed in sheltered bays and certainly could not survive on the

west coast of the island today. Their presence in the midden suggests that the coastal configuration was quite different in Neolithic times. Papa Sound is just over a mile wide and very shallow at its narrowest central part, and possibly, 5500 years ago, Papa Westray was still joined to Westray. There would then have been just the sort of sheltered bay in which oysters might live.

An early Neolithic farm

The reconstruction drawing gives an impression of a Neolithic farm based on Knap of Howar (12). Instead of being in dumps, the midden had been spread out to form a layer of uniform thickness over an area stretching 20m (66ft) to the south of the houses; it seems likely that the object was to use the surface of the midden for intensive cultivation in small plots. Despite the adverse conditions, a few grains of barley and three pollen grains of wheat survived in the soil samples analysed, suggesting that these cereals may have been among the crops grown.

Evidence of manure having been spread on the soil was found at Tofts Ness in Sanday, which supports the idea of intensive cultivation in Neolithic times. At Links of Noltland in Westray, there were traces of the furrows dug into the soil by a primitive type of plough. Arable fields would have been enclosed in some way to keep out animals.

Large quantities of animal bones in the Knap of Howar midden came from domesticated cattle and sheep, apparently bred in equal proportions and mostly slaughtered young. The few pigs, although large and close to their wild counterparts, were probably domesticated as well. All these animals would provide not only meat but a wide range of other products: hides for clothing and bedding, gut for bow-strings and fishing-lines, stomach-bags and bladders for containers, and bone for tool-making. Textiles

12 *Artist's reconstruction of an early Orcadian farming landscape (based on Knap of Howar).*

were unknown in Britain at this period, for the hair of the sheep of the time was unsuitable for spinning.

The opportunities for hunting mammals in the islands would be limited, although a few bones of deer were found. Bones from whales and seals are thought more likely to have been obtained from carcases than from hunting. One of the tools made at Knap of Howar from whalebone resembles the blubber knives used by Eskimos, and it suggests that fresh carcases were sometimes available. Even a small whale would boost the family economy enormously, for the blubber would be a wonderful source of fat, the meat could be dried and stored, and the bones had endless possibilities, from ribs for rafters to trimmed vertebrae as dishes. Among the other whalebone artefacts are a spatula and a mallet-head.

There were plenty of sea-birds to be hunted profitably, such as gannets, fulmars and guille-mots, some of which provided oil as well as meat. The great auk appears to have been a favourite at Knap of Howar; this flightless bird is now extinct, but Papa Westray was evidently a congenial habitat, and sadly the last breeding pair in Scotland was exterminated here in 1813.

Fishing is likely to have played a very import-ant role in the economy in Orkney throughout prehistoric times. The fishbones found in the midden represent both fishing from the shore, using hook and line or baited dropnet to catch young saithe, ballan wrasse and rockling, and offshore fishing from boats, up to 5 miles out to sea, using hook and line to catch large saithe, ling, cod, halibut and turbot. As well as the oysters mentioned already, there was a wide variety of shellfish, including winkles, cockles and razorfish, but by far the most common species was limpets. More than 40,000 shells came from the upper part of the midden, which was contemporary with the two houses. Attempts have been made to assess how useful a food resource limpets were, and it is clear that, compared with meat, they were a poor food in terms of providing energy. One hundred boiled limpets provide only 97.5 calories – and they are so rubbery in texture that it would be difficult to eat very many. In recent centuries in Scotland, they have only become an important food resource in times of severe hardship. They are, however, useful as fishbait, particularly after they have been soaked for some days to soften them. This process could account for the pres-ence of their shells in the midden.

The shells of bivalve molluscs make useful small dishes and scoops, and crushed shell was used as temper to strengthen the clay for pottery-making. A very large quern stood in the inner room of house 1, and beside it were found, during the early excavations, crushed razor-shells, ready perhaps for the potter. Parts of at least 78 pots were recovered from the midden and the house floors, and analysis of the clay used in their manufacture demonstrated that they were made locally in the island. None of the many artefacts need have been imported, includ-ing a small polished axe of local igneous rock. The settlement was entirely self-supporting.

It appears to have been a small farm, the home of generations of an extended family over several hundred years. The two standing buildings were not the first on the site, for there was already a layer of midden into which the houses were dug. The midden became an economical building material, used as wall-core. The builders marked out on the surface of the midden the internal area of each house, and dug out the midden so that the floor of the house was the natural boulder clay and the inner face of the wall made a revetment against the remaining midden. The midden removed from the house floor was then packed down between two stone faces to form a solid and insulating wall-core. It follows that there must have been structures belonging to the time during which this early midden accumulated, but they may have been farther west and destroyed by the sea.

Fortunately, Traill and Kirkness had done little more than clear the sand and rubble out of the two buildings, leaving the floor deposits virtually intact.

Houses at Knap of Howar

Both surviving houses face seawards, each with its main entrance through the west end-wall. This wall was built somewhat thicker than the rest, in order to create a long passage that would help to reduce draughts. The passage into the larger building, house 1, is paved and roofed at a height of 1.3m (4ft) with large flat slabs, and the door stood at the inner end against stone jambs and a sill-stone (13). The door was probably either wooden or a thin flagstone, held in position by a bar. The house is divided into two rooms by a pair of large upright slabs projecting from the side-walls, with a pair of low upright slabs between them. In the gap between each high and low slab is a small pit which originally held a wooden post to help in supporting the roof. The outer room had a paved floor (now gravel) and a low stone bench along one side,

13 Knap of Howar: the dwelling-house was divided into two rooms by upright slabs, and a small side-door led into the workshop.

while the inner room had a clay floor, a hearth and a small shelf built into the wall. Grooves in the floor probably held the supports for a wooden bench, and a large post-hole held another roof-support. The long-vanished roof is likely to have been timber-framed with a covering of turf. A low passage leads through the wall into the adjoining building.

House 2 has a smaller floor-area, 7.5m (25ft) long rather than the 9.5m (31ft) length of house 1, and it is divided into three rooms again by upright slabs (14). The innermost room is furnished with shelves and cupboards built into the thickness of the wall and had a stone-lined pit dug into the clay floor, all presumably for storage. The central room had a thick layer of occupation material and two successive hearths; the earlier hearth was paved and kerbed with stone and is still visible, while the later was simply an ash-filled hollow in the floor, as was that in house 1. The floor deposit yielded a large number of artefacts, including specialized grinding tools. The outer room was little more than a vestibule serving both the main entrance and the

14 *Knap of Howar: the workshop with its central hearth and cupboards built into the wall.*

passage leading into house 1. The presence of jamb-stones at this end of the passage indicated that it could be closed by a door from house 2. The building had evidently gone out of use during the life of house 1, for both entrances had been blocked with stones.

The smaller building has every appearance of being subsidiary, even tacked on, to the larger and more substantially constructed building. This impression, together with the storage facilities and tools found in house 2, led to its interpretation as a workshop attached to a dwelling-house. But there are puzzling aspects. The passage between the two was clearly part of the original design of house 1, yet they were built as separate units with their walls abutting, rather than sharing a common wall. If house 1 was the dwelling-house, why was the door to the passage at the workshop end? Why were both entrances into house 2 carefully sealed with stones? Domestic structures may have had a strong ritual

element in their design and use, which is difficult to recognize but which reflected the beliefs and traditions of their inhabitants. One trace of ritual may be a small pit near the hearth in house 1, which contained a tiny pot and was sealed by a large sherd.

The artefacts appear all to be purely practical, including the very few bone dress-pins, which are basic functional items. The only decoration occurs on the pottery. Skin-working tools are common, including bone awls for making holes, and blunt-ended embossing tools which may imply decoration on clothing. Hammers of whalebone and antler could double up as carpentry tools and flint-working tools. Stone tools include knives and scrapers made from flint and chert, hammerstones made from sandstone beach-pebbles, quern-stones (**15**), pointed tools for boring holes and a unique type of fine grinding-stone.

Knap of Howar in a wider context

The Knap of Howar houses are unusual in their design in Orkney and Shetland, but rectangular houses are typical for this period elsewhere in Scotland and beyond, whether built of stone or wood. Two such houses built side by side at Loch Olabhat in North Uist in the Western Isles are reminiscent of Knap of Howar both in layout and in related pottery; they stood on a small artificial island in the loch, enclosed by a stockade, perhaps introducing an element of defence which is lacking in Orkney. At Balbridie beside the River Dee in north-east Scotland, the post-holes of a magnificent timber house have been excavated; this was almost three times the size of Knap of Howar 1, and easily the largest early Neolithic house in Britain – more like the great wooden longhouses of the early farmers in Europe. The decorated pottery at Balbridie is also related to Unstan Ware.

If rectangular houses were typical of the users of Unstan Ware, more should be found in Orkney when more domestic sites with this pottery are identified. The earliest phase at

Howe, near Stromness, includes the partial remains of two rectangular structures with stone hearths and subdividing upright slabs, which have been variously interpreted as domestic houses and as a mortuary house and a chambered cairn of stalled type. These important excavations have yet to be published, but this phase was clearly succeeded by the construction of a chambered tomb (p.57). Whatever the earliest structures were, their design belongs to the architectural tradition associated with Unstan Ware. The architectural links between houses and burial tombs will be explored in the next chapter.

Until Unstan Ware was found at Knap of Howar, it was known only from the chambered tombs known as stalled cairns, as at Unstan itself, the tomb after which this type of pottery was named. It had seemed possible that this was purely funerary ware, but, once it was discovered in a domestic context, it could be seen as part of an overall cultural assemblage. There is one difference, however, between the pottery in the tombs and that at Knap of Howar. The bowls in the tombs are mostly large and solid, whereas the domestic version is small and finely made. This contrast may reflect the use of large and robust bowls on communal occasions, when they needed to hold greater quantities and withstand handling by many people.

15 *A demonstration of a saddle quern and rubber in use.*

Skara Brae

Every schoolchild in Scotland knows about Skara Brae. It is an astoundingly well-preserved village beneath the turf of the Links of Skaill, where visitors can peer into houses and passages from the level of their roofs (16). But our ground-level is not the ground-level of the inhabitants of Skara Brae, and the village was only latterly and partially subterranean. The story goes back more than 5000 years ago, but our knowledge of it began around 1850, when a severe storm tore the turf from the sand-dunes and exposed the seaward flank of the village.

The landowner was William Watt, who lived in Skaill House overlooking the Bay of Skaill. He and fellow antiquaries explored the ruins on a number of occasions, clearing the sand from the exposed houses and collecting 'relics'. The site was taken into State care in 1924, and in December that year another great storm destroyed much of house 3; it became clear that a sea-wall would have to be built to protect the ruins. At the same time the houses were cleared of debris and the walls consolidated. The help of an archaeologist was needed to deal with the layers of midden, and in 1928 Professor V. Gordon Childe, the holder of the new Abercromby Chair of Archaeology in the University of Edinburgh, accepted the invitation to supervise the work. Childe's own words convey the limited amount of real archaeology that could be achieved during what was essentially a conservation exercise: 'I was privileged to be present during the operations undertaken for the conservation of the remarkable prehistoric village of Skara Brae and to supervise the incidental archaeological results.'

Nevertheless, the work was reasonably successful in unravelling a structural sequence and, from the artefacts, in piecing together a picture of the lifestyle of the inhabitants. The major deficiencies reflect the archaeological techniques of the time, together with the problems of trying to understand the stratigraphy of complex deposits without being able to dismantle stone

16 *The location of Skara Brae on the Bay of Skaill; visitors can look down into some of the houses almost from roof-level.*

structures. The challenge to make good some of the deficiencies was taken up in the 1970s by David V. Clarke, who opened two trenches in areas where intact midden deposits could be expected. One was within the settlement in a triangular area between passages and adjacent to house 7, where the midden was known to be some 4m (13ft) deep. The other was on the northern edge of the settlement, where Childe had encountered very damp midden (**17**). It was thought that the damp conditions might have preserved plant material – and so it proved to be.

Skara Brae is remarkable both for the excellent state of preservation of some of the houses and for the stone-built furniture that is so evocative of domestic life (**colour plate 1**). One reason for the preservation is the fact that the village was blanketed by windblown sand soon after its abandonment. A popular myth would have the village abandoned during a massive storm that threatened to bury it in sand instantly, but the truth is that its burial was gradual and that it had already been abandoned – for what reason, no one can tell. Another factor that ensured its preservation is the presence of deep midden-deposits around the houses and passages.

When rubbish is more than just rubbish

Prior to excavation, the midden at Skara Brae not only cocooned the houses but spread over the top of the roofed passages. Childe described the midden as standing 'to the huts and passages in the same relation as the flesh to the organs and veins of a living body'. He was also convinced that daily activities were carried out on the surface of the midden, to account for the higher numbers of artefacts that were found in the uppermost layer. 'The conclusion is that the surface of their dunghill was utilized by the

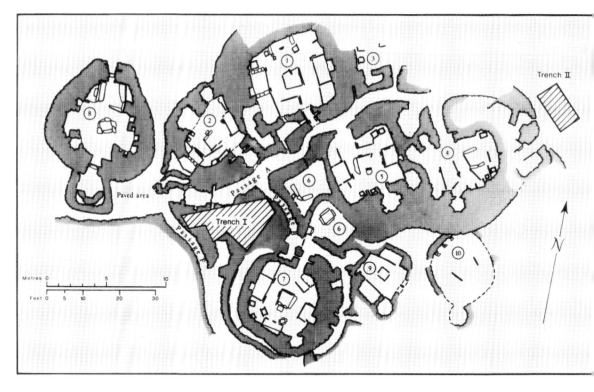

17 *Plan of Skara Brae showing the position of the trenches excavated in the 1970s.*

villagers to live on during fine weather.' This vision of cosy life in and on a steaming rubbish dump is hard to credit, but the evidence cannot be interpreted satisfactorily in any other way. David Clarke has argued that midden was seen by the inhabitants as an essential building material and that the creation of the midden heap was 'the first stage in the construction process'. Once the heap had become stable and solid, houses were built in large pits in the midden, and passages were built in channels created for the purpose (**18**).

Consolidated rubbish was used at this period elsewhere in Orkney and Shetland as a building material, but nowhere to the same extent as at Skara Brae. The houses at Knap of Howar were dug into an existing midden, and the midden was used as wall-core, but it was not used as backing to the walls, despite the fact that there was plenty of material that could have been piled up for that purpose. At Rinyo, the slope of the hillside was

counteracted by the creation of artificial terrace made either of midden or of horizontal stones but the houses were not embedded in midden. A Links of Noltland, a hollow was dug into the sand-dune and lined with midden, as a revetmen against which the walls of the building were constructed. The houses at Barnhouse and Poo were entirely free-standing and lacked any use o midden as a building material. In Shetland midden was used as wall-core at Ness of Gruting but not at the earlier settlement at Scord o Brouster. The desire of the inhabitants of Skara Brae to live partially underground is but one o the curious aspects of this site that may mark i out as special rather than normal.

Skara Brae houses

The appearance of Skara Brae today is some what misleading, in the sense that the visible buildings are not all contemporary. The bes preserved, houses 1–8, are those belonging to the final phases of the settlement (**19**), while between and beneath them are the remains of earlier

houses. Part of an earlier house was found in the lower levels of midden in trench I excavated in the 1970s. Its construction demonstrated how the midden had been used, for it had clearly been built in a hollow scooped into the contemporary surface; the edge of the hollow had been lined with clay as a base for the house wall.

Environmental evidence shows that the village lay in grassland with sand-dunes separating it from the bay. The size of the early settlement is unknown, because much of it lies beneath the later buildings, but the design of the exposed houses, particularly the most complete house, no. 9, appears to have been very similar to that of the later village. At least eight houses belonged to the later village, although they may not all have been in use at the same time, and one or two

18 (Left) *A roofed passage in the late village at Skara Brae.*

19 (Below) *House 1 at Skara Brae.*

others may have been lost into the sea. Radiocarbon dating shows that the lifespan of the settlement was some 600 years, from about 3100 BC to about 2500 BC.

What makes the houses truly remarkable, apart from their excellent preservation, is their stone furniture and their uniform design. Each consists of a single spacious room with one entrance. The walls survive up to 3m (10ft) in height, which implies that the roof was at a level that allowed free movement beneath and storage amongst the rafters. No trace remains of the roof

20 *Artist's reconstruction of the interior of house 1 at Skara Brae.*

itself, but a framework of timber and perhaps whale ribs should be envisaged, with an outer covering of living turf. The floor area of the room is about 36 sq m (388 sq ft), but the available space is limited by a number of permanent fixtures, which set a pattern to the various daily activities (20). The centre of the room is occupied by a substantial square or rectangular hearth with a stone kerb, and each wall, other than that through which the doorway opens, accommodates a major piece of stone-built furniture. Opposite the door is a mighty dresser with two shelves supported by three piers. Between the dresser and the hearth there is sometimes a block of stone, perhaps acting as a 'seat of honour'.

Flanking the hearth on either side is a large box interpreted as a bed; inside there would have been heather and straw as a mattress, and animals skins as coverings. Childe argued that the high corner posts may have supported a skin canopy. In the early houses, these beds are recessed into the walls, but in the later and larger houses they project into the room. Mostly they were made with upright slabs, but the left-hand bed in house 1 has a slab along the front and masonry ends into which shelves were built. More storage space was achieved by building cells and alcoves into the house-wall and by sinking small stone boxes into the floor. The corners of these boxes were sealed with clay to make them watertight, and Childe dubbed them 'limpet boxes'. David Clarke has argued that their purpose may have been not to keep limpets alive as food but to soak them until soft enough to use as fish-bait.

Childe drew attention to the fact that the right-hand bed is always larger than the left. He found beads and paint-pots in some of the smaller beds and suggested that they may have been the women's beds, while the men used the larger beds. In most of the later houses, there is some item of furniture, usually a slab-built box, to the immediate left of the entrance, obliging the person entering to turn to the right into the 'male' area of the house. If this apparent interest in left and right, female and male, is real, it may suggest that one view of the world held by the inhabitants concerned duality, a very common feature of human cosmology.

The cells in house 1 are particularly interesting. On the left of the entrance is a cell from which the bar for the door was operated and which also has a 'peep-hole' into the passage outside. Opening from the wall opposite the door, there were originally two cells, which were destroyed by the sea; one in the north-east corner had a drain leading out under the house-wall, and this Childe interpreted as a lavatory. The other appears to have been a secret place, for its entrance could only be reached by crawling under the dresser. There are also cells served by drains in houses 4 and 5, and Childe viewed these lavatories as 'a sign of hygienic progress and modesty not easily reconcilable with the filth surrounding the huts and covering their floors'. But this sign of hygiene may instead suggest that Childe was mistaken in his image of filth and squalor. The midden outside the houses was after all variable in how much organic matter it contained, and long-rotted compost loses its noxious character and smell. The state of the house-interiors as Childe found them may not reflect normal living conditions. His description seems, in any case, to be exaggerated, for only house 7 contained a high number of artefacts and organic remains.

Cells in houses could clearly have many different functions. What are we to make of the cells that open off communal passages? One opens off the south-west passage that skirts house 7, and it boasts a decorated stone. It was built at a high level into the midden and was unconnected with any house. Another cell opens off the passage on the east side of house 7. Originally a cell opened off the main passage into the wall of house 1, but this was subsequently blocked off and made into an extension of the internal cell in the west wall of the house. No cell shows any sign of having had a door.

On a calm sunlit day, the village conveys a sense of serene unity, the houses clustered closely together and their interiors arranged to a common pattern. On a rough day, with an Atlantic gale sending squalls of rain horizontally across the bay, one appreciates the wisdom of embedding the village in its warm insulating midden. But it is possible to exaggerate the sense of unity, for a dominant architectural feature is the bar-hole set on either side of entrances to secure a door against intruders. Not only could the main passage through the village be sealed in this way, but also the individual houses and probably the side-passages. In addition, there is an important psychological contrast between the inner world and the immediate outside world. Inside the house was a warm and spacious world in which one could move about upright and with ease. But entry to that world was through a doorway so low that one was forced to crouch down to one's knees, and outside the passage was almost as low as well as narrow, winding, and dark.

Superficially, house 7 appears to conform to the other houses, but there are several unique features. Access is down a side-passage, thereby isolating it from the main part of the village. Its door was barred not from the inside but from the outside, from a cell on the right-hand side of the entrance which could only be entered from the passage. Beneath the right-hand bed and wall was discovered a stone-built grave containing the remains of two adult females. It was clear that they had been buried before the house was constructed. This may represent some sort of foundation ritual involved in the process of creating a special building. Several theories have been put forward to explain the purpose of this building, mostly derived from social anthropological data and based on it having been a place of confinement. These range in focus from punishment to meditation, initiation, childbirth and menstruation, all of which may have involved physical separation from the rest of the community.

One other building appears to have been separated deliberately from the main village. This is house 8, which is literally separate in the sense of standing alone and free of any enveloping midden on the west side of the village, and also distinct in its design and function. It lies beyond the west gate of the main passage, on the other side of an open paved area that Childe dubbed the 'Market Place'. The house is oval in shape, both inside and out, and has a small 'porch' added on to one end at the entrance.

There is a central hearth but no dresser, 'limpet boxes' or enclosed beds, although there are large recesses in the side-walls where beds might be expected. There are also shelves and cupboards built into the walls and a small cell to the left of the entrance. Childe called this building 'the industrial quarter', partly because it lacked the design and contents of the domestic houses, and partly because he found, on the floor, ample debris from chert-working.

Access into the building for the modern visitor is through a gap in the north wall, which means that one is seeing it back to front; this part, where normally the dresser would stand, seems to have been a paved working area. In it were many burnt stones, which has suggested to some scholars that the chert was being subjected to heating and cooling in order to improve its flaking qualities. The gap in the house-wall has been interpreted as a flue to aid the heating process, but there is no evidence that the stones were heated in this area rather than in the hearth. The gap may have acted as a service hatch through which stones were passed, fresh on the way in and cracked and burnt on the way out.

Art at Skara Brae

Part of the special status of houses 7 and 8 was expressed through art. These are the only buildings to be embellished by carved patterns on their walls, and house 8 is particularly well-endowed. Art seems to have been more important to the inhabitants of the later village at Skara Brae than to people living anywhere else. Not only are the buildings decorated but also some of the artefacts, whereas elsewhere only pottery seems to have been considered appropriate for ornament. (Orcadian Neolithic art is discussed in chapter 4.) The location of the decoration, together with the stratigraphic evidence for the buildings, suggests that the later village might itself be divided into broadly earlier and later phases in which the art is seen to belong to the final phase (**21**). The earlier core of the village would consist of houses 1, 3, 4 and 5, with a vast

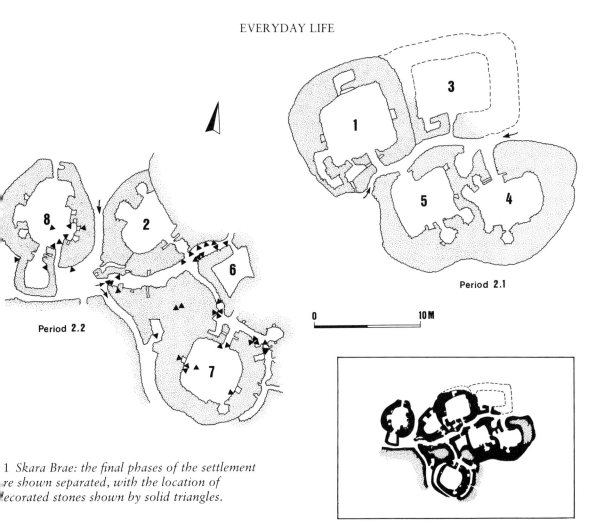

1 *Skara Brae: the final phases of the settlement are shown separated, with the location of decorated stones shown by solid triangles.*

midden heap to the south-west, and houses 2, 6, 7 and 8, together with their associated decoration, would form the final expansion of the village.

Everyday life at Skara Brae

Village economy was very similar to that at Knap of Howar, based on mixed farming and fishing. Cattle, a few pigs, dogs, sheep and goats were bred, and cereal crops were grown, mostly barley but also some wheat. Some deer were hunted, and full use was made of stranded whales. The midden contained vast numbers of limpet-shells and fish-bones, the latter mostly from cod and saithe. As well as bird-bones, some of which were made into awls, small fragments of birds' eggs were recovered, which may indicate that people were collecting eggs as food. It was a self-sufficient community, making pottery and tools and needing to import only haematite to use as a polishing material. Haematite is likely to have come from the island of Hoy.

The type of pottery used at Skara Brae is known today as Grooved Ware, on account of its characteristic grooved decoration. These were flat-bottomed bucket-shaped jars, sometimes in Orkney made of very thick pottery and up to 0.6m (2ft) in diameter. Grooved Ware was used by communities over a very wide area from Orkney to southern England, but it was made locally in popular styles. Some of the Skara Brae vessels had attractive scalloped rims, and applied decoration was common; pellets and cordons of clay were stuck to the outside of the pot before firing, thereby creating chunky patterns of

35

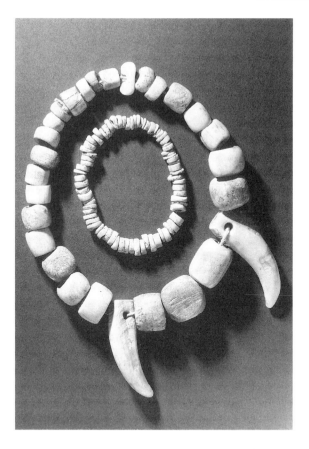

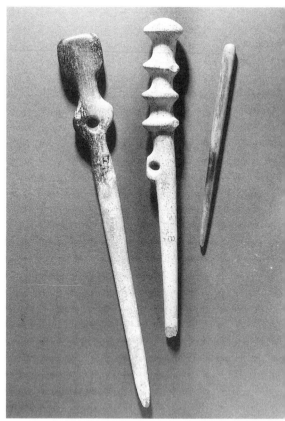

22 (Left) *Bone necklaces from Skara Brae; the stringing is modern.*

23 (Right) *Bone pins from Skara Brae.*

spirals, zig-zag and knobs. There are many links between pottery decoration and the designs used on other artefacts and on stones in buildings and passages in the settlement.

Local chert and beach flint were used extensively for small stone tools such as scrapers. Sandstone pebbles became hammerstones or were flaked to make quick and handy knives, and chunks of igneous camptonite rock were made into axes and balls. Bone was an invaluable and plentiful material for making all manner of tools, from skin-working awls to mattock-heads, decorative pins, pendants and beads (**22, 23**). Some of the decorative items will be discussed in chapter 4. Flint or chert knives were probably used to cut bone, and pumice acted like modern sandpaper to smooth rough edges and sharpen bone points. Plenty of pumice could be found on Orcadian beaches, carried by the sea from Iceland, where it was a by-product of volcanic eruptions.

The waterlogged midden on the northern edge of the settlement yielded a number of pieces of equipment made from plant materials, which under normal soil conditions rot away. These included short lengths of rope made by twisting together stems of heather and a finely carved wooden handle. More unexpected were the remains of ten puff-balls, the fungus *Bovista nigrescens*. Puff-balls are filled with fibrous material almost like cotton-wool, which is known to have been used in relatively recent times to help staunch bleeding and to encourage the blood to clot in wounds. The people of Skara Brae may well have known of this useful property.

Skara Brae provides an unforgettable glimpse

of life 5000 years ago. Gordon Childe can hardly have hoped that another such settlement would be uncovered within a few years.

Rinyo in Rousay

The Grooved Ware settlement at Rinyo was discovered and first excavated by James Yorston, the son of the father and son team of Yorstons who worked on Walter Grant's Trumland estate in the 1930s and 1940s. James Yorston junior found upright slabs protruding through the turf on the lower terraces of Faraclett Head, in an area known as the Braes of Rinyo, and carried out some excavation during the winter of 1937–8. He realised that there were strong architectural and cultural links with Skara Brae, with the result that excavations were renewed in the summer under the direction of Gordon Childe and Walter Grant. War then intervened, and the excavation was resumed and finished in the summer of 1946.

Remains were found of several houses, but only their basal courses survived, partly because the area had been ploughed in modern times, but also because there were no deep deposits of midden or sand to preserve them. Nevertheless, it was clear that there had been a number of episodes of building and that houses had been demolished to make way for new buildings over a long period of time. The design of the houses is very similar to those in the main settlement at Skara Brae, with central hearth, dresser and beds; carefully built drains were again a marked feature. Drainage was a greater problem here, owing to water trickling down from the higher slopes, and the remains of a water-proof lining of hazel-bark was found in one drain. The overall layout of the settlement is uncertain from the limited area excavated, but it is likely to have been strung out along the natural terrace, and it may have been considerably larger than Skara Brae.

The most interesting, and as yet unique, structural feature at Rinyo was the clay oven. It lay adjoining the hearth in one of the houses, and

24 *Rinyo in 1938: one of the clay oven-bases with a 6-inch rule for scale (0.15m).*

it consisted of a flat slab of stone let into the floor and a clay superstructure. On the outside the clay oven was circular, but inside it was 0.37m (1ft 2in) square with rounded corners. It survived to a height of about 0.23m (9in), with an opening on one side, but its original roof was probably dome-shaped. The stone base was hollowed out over the interior area of the oven, and two similar slabs were discovered elsewhere in the settlement (**24**), implying that this was not the only oven. But what were they used for and how were they heated? There was no trace of fire within the oven, but hot pebbles from the hearth may have been placed on the base slab. Perhaps these little ovens were used for baking bread.

The domestic equipment used by the inhabitants of Rinyo is very similar to that at Skara Brae. Soil conditions were such that very little bone survived, but there is ample pottery with applied and grooved decoration, along with small flint tools, polished stone axes and a broken macehead, plain stone balls, lumps of haematite polished by use, 'Skaill knives', stone pot-lids, small stone vessels and saddle querns. The use of bone pins and awls is implied by the presence of many pieces of pumice with grooves worn by sharpening the points of such implements.

Recent discoveries of Grooved Ware settlements

Be these surmises as they may,
I one time went to Scarabrae
To view with antiquarian dream
The prehistoric housing scheme.

Thus wrote Robert Rendall, who went on to dream of life among the flint-workers and 'mussel-pudding makers'. The idea of a housing scheme or a row of identical houses is familiar in the modern world, where it represents normally the output of one building company repeating for economy's sake one architectural design. This is unlikely to have been the explanation at Skara Brae and Rinyo, although the existence of a specialist class of builders cannot be ruled out. The adoption and repetition of one particular design for houses – and, as we shall see in the next chapter, particular designs for tombs – would have been part of the complex beliefs and customs of the time. After the excavation of Rinyo, some thirty years were to pass before any other Neolithic houses were identified in Orkney, and, when they were found, the pattern was broken. Despite the fact that their inhabitants used Grooved Ware and other artefacts similar to those at Skara Brae and Rinyo, the buildings at Links of Noltland in Westray did not conform to the same blueprint. They may not be typical of the original settlement, however, for the excavations in 1978–80 uncovered only part of an extensive area of sand-dunes which may hide many other buildings. The excavator, David Clarke, has estimated that this village may have been four times the known size of Skara Brae. The lobate plan of the excavated building resembles closely the chambered tomb at Vinquoy in Eday, and there was evidence of careful and selective infilling of the Noltland building which may suggest that its purpose was more than simply domestic (**25** i–j).

Nevertheless, the Skara Brae-Rinyo pattern re-emerged with excavations in the 1980s at Pool in Sanday and at Barnhouse in mainland Orkney. The very location of Barnhouse gives it additional importance, for it is no more than a few minutes' walk from the contemporary ceremonial monument known as Stones of Stenness (pp.73–8) and both are part of the complex late Neolithic landscape centred on the lochs of Harray and Stenness. It lies beside the southern end of the Loch of Harray on flat ground. Fieldwalking by Colin Richards and his team has identified other inland lochside settlements of this period. Previously the distribution of early settlement had appeared to be predominantly coastal, but it is now clear that this was an accident of discovery through coastal erosion.

The remains of 15 houses of several phases were uncovered at Barnhouse, but only part of the settlement was excavated and the total number of buildings is unknown. The houses were built free-standing without any obvious indication of passage-ways between them, and it is not known whether there was any form of enclosure round the settlement which might have taken the place of the protective gates at Skara Brae. Externally the houses would have appeared circular, their walls clad with turf on the outside and a good stone face on the inside. The roofs are thought to have been of turf on a timber frame. As at Skara Brae and Rinyo, Barnhouse has examples both of beds set into the thickness of the wall and of beds against the wall; there is a square stone hearth in the centre of each house, and a stone dresser against the back wall opposite the entrance (**25** b).

Two of the buildings are large and more complex in design. House 2 appears to be a double version of the normal house, rather better

25 *Plans of early houses: a, Skara Brae 7; b, Barnhouse 3; c, Rinyo G; d, Knap of Howar 1; e, Loch Olabhat A; f, Howe; g, Skara Brae 8; h, Gruting School 1; i, Links of Noltland; j, Vinquoy tomb.*

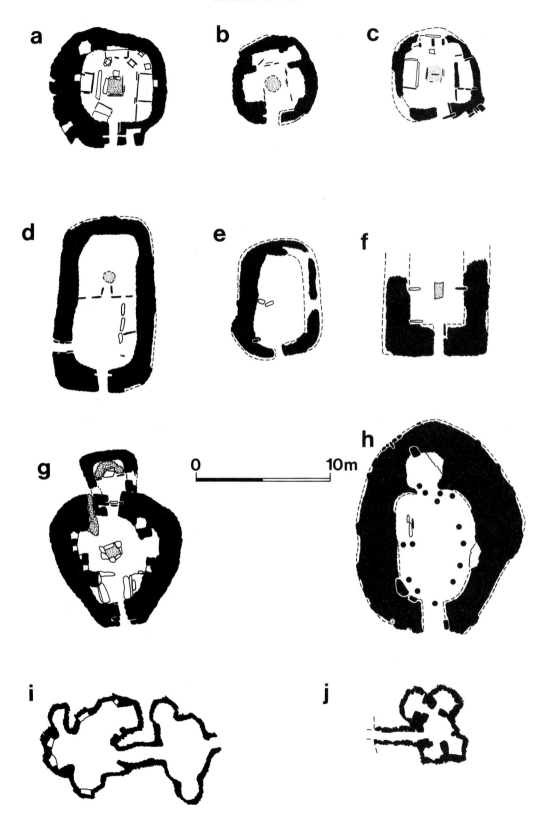

built, with an outer wall-face enclosing a clay core and a precisely designed inner face creating six rectangular recesses. But the two hearths, one in each half of the building, were not in fact contemporary, rather the one to the right of the entrance was replaced by that to the left. Colin Richards has suggested that the recesses were not beds. He has drawn attention to the close resemblance of this building to the tombs at Quanterness and Quoyness. Whereas other houses were replaced by new versions during the lifetime of the settlement, house 2 remained standing throughout the entire period. Built at a later date than house 2 is an extraordinary structure, 8, described by its excavator as monumental; here a square room, fully 7m (23ft) across within a 3m (10ft) thick wall, was furnished with a massive central hearth and rear dresser. It was set on a circular platform of yellow clay which was itself enclosed by a thick stone wall. The entrance to this building faces north-west and may be aligned on the midsummer sunset. In keeping with the special character of the building, the entrance was 3m (10ft) long and elaborate in design, flanked by upright stones and containing a hearth.

It is difficult to know how to interpret these two buildings; if they were domestic houses, they could be seen as the prestigious homes of successive chieftains, or, if their function was more formal, they could be interpreted as communal meeting-houses.

Some years ago, Euan MacKie interpreted Skara Brae as a special housing unit for an élite class of priests whose task was to officiate at ceremonies at Stones of Stenness and Brodgar. For several reasons this idea failed to find acceptance amongst archaeologists, but it is an idea which could now be applied instead to the two special buildings at Barnhouse, if not to the entire settlement. Barnhouse is at least conveniently close to the Stenness-Brodgar ceremonial centre, and the entrance into the monumental structure 8 is remarkably similar to the internal design of the Stones of Stenness.

Barnhouse has yet to be published in full, but the pottery is Grooved Ware and close in character to pottery both from Stones of Stenness and from Skara Brae. There is an extensive flint and stone assemblage, including pitchstone from the island of Arran in western Scotland. Soil conditions were unfortunately unsuitable for the preservation of bonework.

At Barnhouse, houses appear to have been deliberately demolished at the end of their lifespan; indeed, so little survives of any of the buildings that the settlement as an entity is likely to have been demolished when, for whatever reason, it was abandoned. Similar acts of demolition can be detected at Skara Brae and Rinyo. Colin Richards has argued that, at Barnhouse, the lifespan of the house was linked to that of its inhabitants and their kinship group. Previously, Audrey Henshall had suggested that material from middens or from house floors was taken into chambered tombs as part of the funerary ritual, to account both for the black soil found on chamber floors and for the inconsequential assortment of flint tools contained within the soil. If these two ideas are combined, it might be possible to envisage a complex ceremony or series of ceremonies involving a final cleaning of the house floor prior to its demolition and the sprinkling of that soil and rubbish within the family tomb. Logically this could not happen every time there was a death, but it could be associated with the death of a particularly important person or with the end of a particular phase in the history of the family or kinship group.

CHAPTER THREE

Ancestral celebrations

A short crossing in a boat takes the modern visitor to the Holm of Papa Westray, but in Neolithic times it may have been possible to walk there. Even in modern times, exceptionally low tides have allowed people to wade across from the rocky point at the north end of South Wick to the rocks engagingly known as Dog Bones at the north end of the Holm (**26**). Erosion by North Sea waves combined with rising sea-level has detached what was once a promontory on the coast of Papa Westray. Ponies were kept on the island at one time, but it is now the province of sheep and guillemots, the one to graze and the other to nest and breed along the rocky east coast. This tiny island is also host to two or possibly three Neolithic tombs, despite the fact that none has been found on Papa Westray itself. Once Knap of Howar had been identified as a Neolithic farm, the question arose as to whether any of the tombs on the Holm might have belonged to the people who lived at the farm.

One of the three tombs is a vast and extraordinary structure. The long oblong mound was opened in 1849 by Captain F.W.L Thomas with the help of the crew of H.M. Cutter *Woodlark*, and it was found to cover a very long chamber with 12 side-cells and an entrance passage (see **34** B). It was taken into State care in 1930, when a concrete roof was built over the chamber; access is through a hatch in the roof, and from a distance the mound resembles a submarine with its conning-tower. This modern access is considerably easier than the original design, which involved crawling along a tunnel only 0.8m (2ft 8in) high. The main chamber was originally almost 3m (10ft) high and is fully 13.5m (44ft) long. Access into the end-chambers and side-cells is again through low and narrow openings, only 0.4m to 0.6m (2ft) high (**colour plate 4**). This type of tomb, with a rectangular or square chamber and side-cells, is known today as the Maes Howe-type, after Maes Howe in mainland Orkney, but this example on the Holm of Papa Westray is by far the most exaggerated version of the design. As the plan shows, in effect, it consists of two Maes Howe-type tombs linked by a central long chamber. Captain Thomas found no artefacts, but George Petrie recorded a number of decorated stones in the walls of the main chamber and the end-chambers (p.67). Decoration is confined to this type of tomb, and elsewhere in Orkney such tombs are associated with pottery and artefacts belonging to the Grooved Ware community.

This tomb at the south end of the island is thus unlikely to have been built or used by the people from Knap of Howar, who used the distinctively decorated Unstan bowls. Unstan ware was named after the tomb at Unstan near Stromness and has been found in a number of other tombs, all characterized by another architectural design known as a stalled cairn. Here the main chamber is divided up into burial compartments by pairs of upright slabs, just as the houses at Knap of Howar are divided into rooms by pairs of slabs.

26 *Aerial view of the Holm of Papa Westray, with the south tomb in the foreground. In the background can be seen the skerries between the Holm and Papa Westray, which are uncovered at low tide.*

The stalled cairn is at the north end of the island (27) and was first excavated by George Petrie over a few days in 1854. He recorded a rectangular chamber divided into three compartments, in which he found human bones and deer tines. His drawing seemed to suggest that there might be a fourth compartment, still intact, as well as an entrance passage. This was enough to justify another excavation, especially if a link with Knap of Howar could be proved.

Work began under the direction of the author in July 1982, and the first surprise was that Petrie had left behind the bones that he had found, apart from one skull which he had presented to the Museum in Edinburgh. This meant that a reasonably accurate estimate could be made of the number of people whose bones remained in the tomb. The second surprise was that he had not cleared out the three compartments down to the floor, with the result that there was still an undisturbed basal layer, with more bones and a number of artefacts. The entrance passage and its ancient filling were still intact. The hypothetical fourth compartment proved to exist and to contain not only more burials but a special deposit of fish-bones. But the greatest surprise was that the end-wall of the chamber consisted not of the usual large upright slab but of a blocked-up entrance.

It was only a small team (the nine people who could fit into the boat for the daily crossing to the island) and funding was limited. The sealed entrance was gradually uncovered during the

27 *Looking down the passage into the stalled chamber at Holm of Papa Westray North.*

excavation of the fourth compartment, and time ran out before it could be investigated. The tomb had to be backfilled until they could return the following summer. Speculation as to what might lie behind that walling was fuelled by the fact that there was no precedent for such an entrance, blocked up during the original use of the tomb.

The team returned on 5 July 1983, but there were still other tasks to be done before they could make a start on the sealed entrance. On Monday 11 July, a day of thick sea-mist and drizzling rain, they took the turf off the cairn at the back of the chamber to expose the top of what appeared to be a circular cell with a corbelled roof. It was filled with earth and organic material, which meant that the cell would have to be excavated horizontally, dismantling the walling in the entrance course by course as the filling was removed. This was in fact the reverse of the procedure by which the cell had been filled and sealed.

Considerable care had gone into the filling. There were several distinct layers, each characterized by different organic remains. The top layer contained limpet shells and deer tines, the second layer contained human bones, sheep and otter bones and deer tines, the third human, sheep and otter bones with an emphasis upon skulls, and the basal layer consisted of large stones intermixed with the bones of sheep, deer and otter. Beneath that, nothing. The floor of the cell was bare (**28**).

How had it been used and why was it so important to fill and close it with such care and deliberate selection of material? The cell was the very first element of the tomb to be built, for it was enclosed within its own small cairn of stones before the main chamber was added, and the stratigraphy of the main chamber showed clearly that the cell had been sealed off early in the use of the rest of the tomb. Some of the human bones in the cell belonged to the same individuals as bones found in the main chamber.

The only ways in which this tomb could be linked firmly with Knap of Howar were through pottery and radiocarbon dating. What was needed were the finely decorated Unstan bowls found in the settlement and radiocarbon dates contemporary with the settlement. Instead there were sherds of plain bowls, but there were dates from human bones at around 3200 BC, which means that the tomb was in use during the later phase of occupation of the settlement. The link is thus possible but not proven!

Houses of the dead

In the report on the tomb at Blackhammer in Rousay that was published in 1937, chambered tombs were aptly described as 'elaborately constructed houses for the dead'. More recently it has been realized that there is more truth to this than a simple metaphor. There are direct architectural links between tombs and domestic houses, and in many ways the 'houses of the dead' mirror closely the houses of the living. The

28 The empty cell at Holm of Papa Westray North.

similarity in overall design can be seen in the drawing (**29**). The Knap of Howar house is rectangular with rounded corners, and the space inside is divided into three rooms by pairs of upright slabs, while the stalled cairn at Yarso shares the same shape and the chamber is similarly divided into four compartments, or, more strictly, four pairs of compartments. The Skara Brae house is square inside and rounded outside, and there are entrances into storage cells built within the thickness of the wall, while at Wideford the Maes Howe-type chamber is set within a round cairn and side-cells open off the chamber. In all cases entrances are low, and this aspect is exaggerated in Skara Brae houses and Maes Howe tombs, sometimes to the extent that visitors are forced to their knees to gain entry. The contrast is then all the greater when the entrance opens into a spacious house or a lofty burial chamber.

The similarities between houses and tombs extend beyond the overall design. The walling between the uprights is sometimes bowed

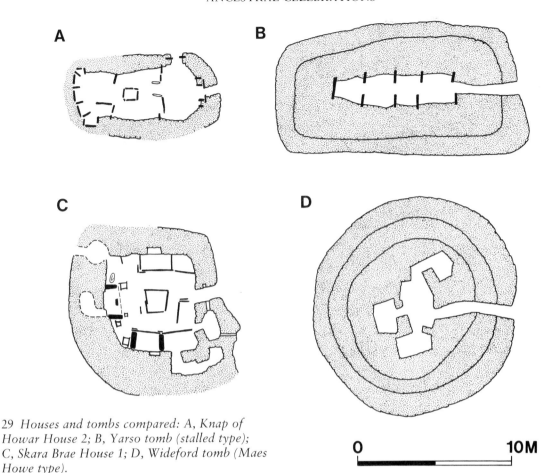

29 *Houses and tombs compared: A, Knap of Howar House 2; B, Yarso tomb (stalled type); C, Skara Brae House 1; D, Wideford tomb (Maes Howe type).*

0   10M

outwards as a device to strengthen the structure. Stone-built benches furnish several stalled tombs, and both stone and wooden benches lined the walls of house 1 at Knap of Howar. The innermost space is often the most complex in function; the innermost room in Knap of Howar 2 has shelves and cupboards built into the walls and a pit dug into the floor, and the innermost compartment of several tombs display shelves, boxes or special arrangements of bones.

The idea of building tombs to resemble the houses of the living is unlikely to have been simply a response to a desire for a familiar resting-place. Unlike the burial traditions of later times, no personal belongings were placed alongside the dead to ensure that life after death could carry on in much the same way as before. As far as we can judge, death in Neolithic times

created ancestors, not just literally but in the sense that the dead were seen in relation to the living rather than as being on their way to somewhere else. Ancestors represented the rights of the living to their land and social allegiances. Their bones could be manipulated to suit the purposes of the living. Very few complete skeletons have been found in the tombs, and it is clear that bones were re-arranged and some even removed after interment. The ancestors were no longer individual people but corporate gatherings.

There is, as described in the last chapter, a growing body of evidence to suggest that there was more to building a domestic house than the simple creation of a sheltered space. The ritual concepts behind the design and use of both houses and tombs were part of contemporary

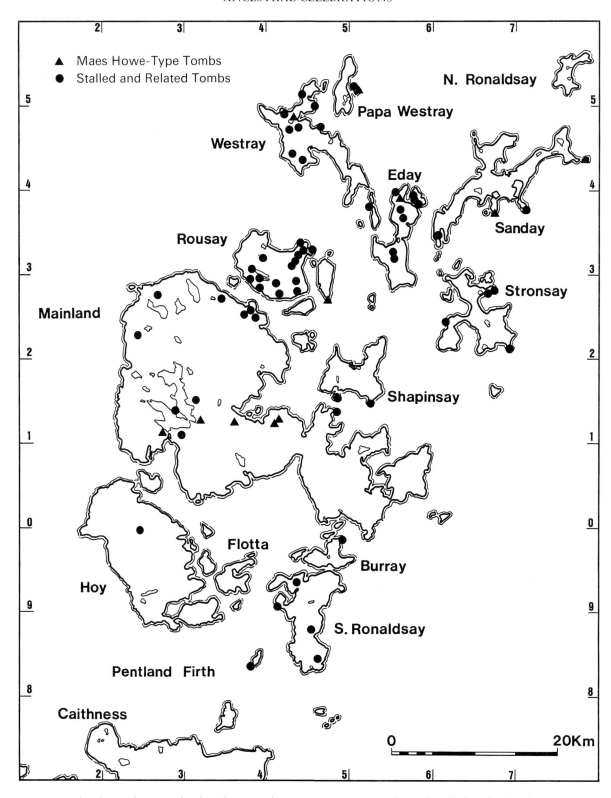

30 *Map of Orkney showing the distribution of Maes Howe-type tombs and stalled and related tombs.*

cosmology, of the way in which people viewed the world around them and their relationship to it.

Throughout Scotland, burial monuments are by far the most numerous surviving remains of Neolithic communities. One scholar and field-worker has made the study of chambered tombs her own by virtue of the encompassing scale of her work and unparalleled first-hand knowledge of her subject. Audrey Henshall published two companion volumes on *The Chambered Tombs of Scotland* in 1963 and 1972, and she has since embarked on a regional revision, first Orkney, then Caithness and currently Sutherland. There are some 80 chambered tombs in Orkney, but the distribution map (30) includes only those identified by Audrey Henshall as certain or probable examples of either stalled and related cairns or of Maes Howe-type cairns. There are only 10 undoubted tombs of the Maes Howe-class, against five times as many stalled or related tombs. This numerical difference will be discussed below in terms of dating and the labour involved in their construction. The surviving pattern of distribution of all known tombs suggests that this is only the remnant of the original total, and that nineteenth-century improvements in agricultural techniques may have been responsible for the destruction of many cairns. The distribution is biased towards land that is marginal in the sense of having little agricultural potential. Coastal erosion may also have taken a toll, for a quarter of the surviving tombs are situated on or close to the modern coastline.

The earliest tombs in Orkney are likely to be those closest in design to early tombs in Caithness, on the grounds that the first farmers in the islands most probably crossed the Pentland Firth from the nearest coast of mainland Scotland. Interpretation of the surviving distribution of tombs in Caithness is beset by similar problems to those in Orkney. There are only three tombs surviving along the coast between Thurso and Duncansby Head, and none has been excavated. Nevertheless, the known early tombs in Caithness as a whole have small chambers, divided into two or three compartments by pairs of upright slabs. The Grey Cairns of Camster, for instance, display tripartite chambers as well as a more unusual small single-compartment chamber. In Orkney, tripartite chambers such as that at Bigland Round in Rousay, and the related variant design known as the Bookan type, are thought to be among the earliest tombs.

A two-storey example of the Bookan type can be seen in Rousay at Taversoe Tuick (31). It crowns a knoll near Trumland House, and it was discovered to be a tomb in 1898 when the landowner, General Frederick Traill-Burroughs, and his wife decided to create a sheltered garden-seat in the mound. Lady Burroughs was fascinated by the tomb, and she kept a journal over the three weeks during which it was excavated. 'When I went to bed that night I could think of nothing else! There had we sat, during many happy summers, stretched on the purple heather,

31 *Inside the two-storey tomb at Taversoe Tuick.*

basking in the sunshine; laughing and talking with the carelessness of youth, little dreaming that barely eight feet below us sat these grim and ghastly skeletons.'

A later landowner, Walter Grant, gave Taversoe Tuick to the nation and re-excavated the tomb in the 1930s, and it is now roofed with a concrete dome. The design of the tomb is very ingenious. The lower chamber was built below ground-level with an entrance passage leading in from the slope of the knoll on the south, whereas the upper chamber was built at ground-level, immediately above the lower chamber, with a separate entrance passage to the north. There were crouched skeletons on stone benches in the lower chamber, and it was these that Lady Burroughs had glimpsed and thought to be sitting. This remarkable two-storey tomb was then enclosed within a round cairn.

Choice of location

Many tombs appear to have been deliberately built in the most prominent and visible locations available in the area, not necessarily the very tops of hills. In Eday, the tomb on Vinquoy Hill was placed not at the highest point but a little below, where it is visible not only from most of the northern part of Eday but also from Westray and Sanday. On the east side of Mainland Orkney, a semi-circle of hills forms a huge natural amphitheatre overlooking the Bay of Firth, and the tombs at Cuween and Wideford (32, 33) are set on the hillsides on either side of the amphitheatre. Detailed analysis of the location of tombs by David Fraser suggests that their builders were most concerned with achieving maximum visibility over an area from half to 3 miles away. This implies that the community responsible for each tomb was living and working within easy walking distance of the tomb.

The island of Rousay has become a favourite target for spatial analysis since Gordon Childe first drew attention to the close similarity between the distribution of cairns and the settlement pattern of the nineteenth century.

Later analyses have emphasized this correlation between the cairns and the cultivatable land, and they have been used to argue that each cairn was sited to overlook the territory exploited by its builders. On the basis of the evidence from Quanterness, Colin Renfrew suggested that an average community using a chambered cairn might be around 20. There are 15 tombs in Rousay, a figure which would indicate a total population of around 300 people in Neolithic times, compared with about 770 people in the late eighteenth century and 237 in 1961. Compared with other parts of Orkney, this density of tombs in an island only 19 sq miles in extent suggests that few tombs have been lost and that such estimates of population are justifiable. The doubtful factor is the size of the group of people represented by each tomb, for the numbers of surviving bones vary enormously (p.62).

Building a chambered tomb

The first step in building a chambered tomb was to remove the turf and soil and, if necessary, to level the surface of the boulder clay or rock. At Quanterness, the top of a knoll was quarried to create a level circular platform, while at Cuween the chamber and side-cells were cut into the bedrock of a hillside. The ground-plan of the chamber would then have been marked out in some way and building would begin. At Holm of Papa Westray North, where the tomb was aligned along the contour of a very slight slope, the floor-area inside the stalled chamber was levelled after the construction of the walls had begun, leaving the west wall on a small scarp of boulder clay.

The most logical way to construct a stalled chamber would be to start at the inner end by

32 (Top) *The cairn at Wideford displays the outer wall-face and two inner revetment walls which may not originally have been visible.*

33 (Bottom) *A superb example of a corbelled roof over one of the side-cells at Wideford.*

placing into position the large upright slab which normally forms the end-wall, and supporting it behind by stones and in front by the basal courses of the side-walls. Slots would then be dug to take the pairs of upright slabs intended to form the burial compartments on either side of the chamber, and a few courses of walling would be built between the slabs once they were in position. Each slab would project both forwards into the chamber and backwards into the wall. The inner part of the walls of the entrance passage would be built against the two portal slabs, and, because the passage roof would be lower than that of the chamber, it would be roofed at this stage with thick slabs set on end. The side-walls of the chamber could then be built to their full height, and the upper courses would oversail one another slightly, in order to reduce the width that the roofing lintels would have to span. These lintels were laid horizontally, and the internal height of the chamber was probably 3m (10ft) or less. By now the chamber and passage were enclosed within a cladding of cairn, and the final act was to add an another cladding, which had the effect of enlarging the cairn and lengthening the entrance passage. The outer wall-face was often of very high quality, sometimes decorative, with a projecting basal plinth.

At Quanterness, the excavation revealed the sequence of construction of a Maes Howe-type tomb. After the site had been levelled and the plan marked out, the basal course of very large blocks was dragged into place, creating the foundation for both chamber and entrance passage, and at the same time the paving slabs of the passage were laid. The walls and inner cairn were then built up to a height of perhaps a metre (3ft), at which point the next skin of cairn material was begun; the walls and inner cairn could then be raised another metre or so, followed by the raising of the next skin and the start of the outer skin. During the building process, the profile of the cairn would thus be stepped, thus making it easier to raise the large lintel-slabs for the roof, but the final profile

would be rounded above a vertical outer face. In some cases, the chamber roofs were very high, up to 4m (13ft), while at Maes Howe itself it has been estimated that the height could have been as much as 6m (20ft). Audrey Henshall has compared the appearance of the chambers at Quanterness and Quoyness to that of 'the interior of the chimneys which rise from great medieval fireplaces'.

Midhowe stalled cairn

There are more chambered tombs in the island of Rousay than in any other area of equivalent size in Orkney. All 15 cairns are of the stalled variety or related forms such as the two-storey Bookan-type tomb at Taversoe Tuick. Thanks to the work of Walter Grant in the 1930s, several have been excavated and four were found to be so well preserved that they were taken into State care: Midhowe, Taversoe Tuick, Blackhammer and Knowe of Yarso. Midhowe was excavated on behalf of Grant in the summers of 1932 and 1933 by the father and son team of James K. Yorston and James Yorston, both of whom worked for Grant's Trumland estate and carried out a number of excavations for him. The long mound covering the tomb lay on the south-west coast of the island, some 20m (33yds) from the sea on a gentle slope. After the excavation, a hangar-like building was erected over the entire tomb for protection (see 5).

If Holm of Papa Westray South is an exaggerated example of a Maes Howe-type tomb, Midhowe is an equally exaggerated example of a stalled cairn (34). The majority of stalled cairns are divided into four, five or seven compartments, but Midhowe boasts a magnificent 12 along a chamber 23.4m (77ft) in length. One other cairn, Knowe of Rowiegar, was badly disturbed but may also have had 12 compartments, while Knowe of Ramsay proved to have 14 (both cairns are situated along the same coastal strip of Rousay as Midhowe and Knowe of Yarso). Midhowe is preserved to a greater height than others of its class, for its walls

A

B

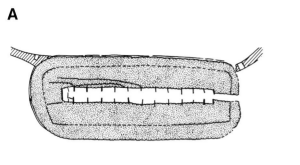

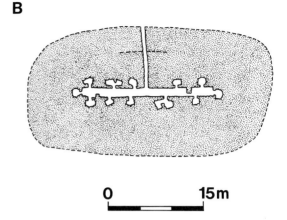

34 *Plans of the tombs at Midhowe (A) and Holm of Papa Westray South (B).*

0   15m

survive up to 2.5m (8ft). The outer wall-face was built in a decorative fashion, with two courses of slabs laid slanting so as to create a herringbone effect (35).

Midhowe is particularly interesting for the furnishing of its interior and for the disposition of its burials. Low stone benches had been built along the east side of the chamber, but not in every compartment, only in the fifth to eleventh compartments. The final compartment had been divided into two by low upright slabs and the innermost section was paved with stones. Bones belonging to 25 people were found, mostly on

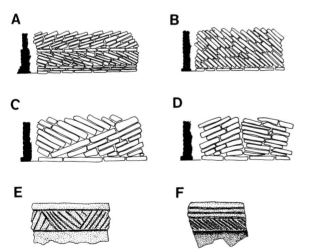

35 *Decorative stonework on stalled cairns (A, Midhowe; B, Yarso; C–D, Blackhammer) compared with decoration on Unstan Ware (E–F).*

the benches, with the exception of the bench in compartment 11 which was bare (36). In most cases, the bones were in heaps, but there were also eight relatively complete skeletons; these represented bodies which had been placed on the benches on their left or right sides, with their legs drawn up to their chests and their backs against the wall so that they faced into the chamber. There was also a deposit of mixed bones beneath the bench in compartment 6, which proved to be the partial remains of two adults and a child. Two skulls were found on the paving on the east side of the innermost part of compartment 12, and the sole burial deposit on the western side of the chamber consisted of a few bones of an adult in compartment 8. Both sides of the first four compartments were empty. Sherds of pottery and a flint knife were found in the west side of the seventh compartment, and more pottery in the east side of the eighth.

Once the decision had been made to close the tomb forever, the entrance passage was blocked by walling at both the inner and outer ends, and the chamber was filled with earth and stones.

Unstan stalled cairn

The tomb of Unstan has been mentioned several times as the site after which were named the finely decorated pottery bowls which have been found in a number of chambered tombs and at

36 *The main chamber at Midhowe; a modern walkway for visitors oversails the tomb.*

the farmstead of Knap of Howar. It was built on a low promontory which projects into the Loch of Stenness in Mainland Orkney, less than a mile from the settlement at Howe. The tomb itself was excavated in 1884 and taken into State care in 1934, after which a concrete dome was built to protect the chamber. Unlike most stalled tombs, which have oblong or rectangular cairns, the cairn at Unstan is circular, because it covers not just a chamber but also a side-cell. In this respect, Unstan is a hybrid architectural design, combining a stalled chamber with a side-cell more typical of Maes Howe-type tombs (**37**). The main chamber is divided into five compartments, of which two are end-compartments because the entrance passage opens not into one end of the chamber like the normal stalled tomb but into one long side of the chamber, again a trait of

Maes Howe tombs. The end-chambers appear to have been furnished with high shelves, because slabs project from the side-walls at a height of about 1.2m (4ft) and are best interpreted as supports for a horizontal flagstone. The floors of these compartments were originally paved behind the low sill-stones that survive at their entrances.

The entrance to the side-cell has been reconstructed in modern times; originally the slabs at either side were not vertical but leaned outwards, like those at the entrance to the end-cell at Holm of Papa Westray North.

Human and animal bones and an unusually large quantity of pottery were found on the floor throughout the tomb. Like Midhowe, there were also crouched skeletons, some in the chamber in the compartment into which the passage opens and two in the side-cell; these represented the latest burials to have been placed there before the tomb was finally closed. Unfortunately this

37 *The main chamber and entrance to the side-cell
at Unstan.*

useful assemblage of human bones was not examined at the time of the excavation, and only a few bones survive, with the result that nothing is known of how many people were buried in the tomb. The many sherds of pottery came from no fewer than thirty bowls. Taversoe Tuick can boast almost as large a collection of Unstan ware, but Isbister yielded even more, some 45 vessels. Most excavated tombs have proved to contain far less pottery, and the difference is clearly not the effect of old and modern techniques of excavation but a genuine reflection of the original activities that went on in the tombs.

Isbister stalled cairn

An extraordinary chance led to the discovery of the chambered tomb of Isbister in 1958. One summer's evening, the farmer, Ronald Simison,

38 *The tomb at Isbister during excavation in the 1980s.*

was walking over a mound near the cliffs when he noticed that part of a wall had been exposed. He pulled away some of the turf and stones to reveal the face of the wall and came across a cache of beautiful objects. There were three fine axe-heads, two made of greenish-brown stone and one of shiny black haematite, and a superb macehead made of speckled black and white stone, polished to a high gloss. There was also a flat oval piece of limestone, shaped ready for its edges to be flaked as a knife, and a round button carefully fashioned from black jet. Later excavation of the entire cairn showed this valuable little hoard to have been placed on the plinth at the base of the outer wall-face of a well-preserved stalled cairn.

Despite the interest that the initial discovery aroused amongst archaeologists as well as amongst Orcadians, the years passed without any formal, professional excavation of the site, owing to lack of funding in an era when resources were being swallowed by rescue

projects on sites threatened by destruction. Eventually in the 1970s Ronald Simison undertook the excavation himself, having first observed the professional excavation by John Hedges of another site on his land (p.94). The full story of how the excavation came about was told by Hedges in *Tomb of the Eagles*, along with his own stimulating ideas about how Neolithic society developed in the third millennium BC. The care of the site has since been taken over by Orkney Islands Council as an important part of the Orcadian heritage, and a roof has been constructed to protect the chamber.

Like Unstan, Isbister is an architectural hybrid. The chamber is divided by pairs of upright slabs into five compartments, and three cells open off the main chamber (38). The entire structure was originally covered by an oval cairn. The end-compartments are very similar to those at Unstan, with sill-stones demarcating their paved floors from that of the central part of the chamber, and high shelves.

The side-cells on the west side of the chamber were intact, and they were roofed at a height of only about 1m (3ft). The main chamber had clearly been filled with earth and stones and midden material when the tomb was closed for the last time, but the cells were left unfilled. The two intact cells contained mostly human skulls. On the floor and particularly along the side-walls of the main chamber was a mass of human bones, which gave the impression of being in small heaps, each with a skull (39). On analysis, the heaps proved not to represent single individuals but parts of several. Altogether, remains of some 338 people had been placed in the tomb. There were also bones from at least 11 people in the filling of the chamber, along with bones of at least 8 white-tailed eagles and a few other birds.

Maes Howe

Most tombs are impressive in one way or another, but Maes Howe is superb. Its size and architectural sophistication combine to make it one of the greatest achievements of neolithic

39 *Isbister: part of the burial deposit in the main chamber.*

builders. Its nineteenth-century excavator was more interested in the runic inscriptions on its walls than in the structure itself (p.9), but he had no means of knowing the great age of this marvellous building. Maes Howe was constructed on flat land near the south end of the Loch of Harray at a time when the Stones of Stenness were already standing a short distance to the west, and the area was becoming the ceremonial heartland of Neolithic Orkney (40). There is no precise scientific dating for the construction of Maes Howe, but scholars are agreed that it should be seen as the culmination of years of building experience rather than as one of the earliest of its type to be built. Radiocarbon dates from the Maes Howe-type tomb at Quanterness have indicated that it was in use by 3000 BC, and a date of around 2800 BC or a little earlier has been hazarded for Maes Howe itself.

The tomb is surrounded by a shallow ditch and low bank (41), across which Gordon Childe and Colin Renfrew excavated trenches in the 1950s and 1970s respectively. Childe had found

40 *The great mound of Maes Howe with the hills
of Hoy in the distance like a gateway to the south.*

41 *Maes Howe from the air.*

peat in the ditch, and Renfrew hoped to obtain radiocarbon dates from that peat, which might help both to date the monument and to reconstruct the contemporary natural environment. His results suggested that Maes Howe had been built on a natural knoll in an open landscape characterized by grassland, with a few cultivated fields and some heathland in the vicinity. Sometime before about 2700 BC, the knoll had been cleared of vegetation and its top levelled ready to build the tomb.

A geophysical survey in 1990 of the area between the tomb-mound and the ditch indicated that beneath the turf were remains of unsuspected features. A small excavation by Colin Richards revealed a stone-lined pit, which is likely once to have held a large standing stone.

42 *The entrance-passage into Maes Howe seen from inside the chamber.*

This survey and excavation suggest that there is still a lot to be learned about Maes Howe, and that its original appearance may have been very different.

The chamber and passage are enclosed within a great mound consisting of a stone core thickly covered with clay and stones. Owing to the nineteenth-century excavations, the mound is now oval, but it is likely originally to have been circular, about 38m (125ft) in diameter and some 8m (26ft) high. The only other tomb of this type which is known to have had an outer clay casing was at Howe, some 3 miles to the south-west, but there it was retained within a thick stone wall. A pit thought to have held a large standing stone was also found at Howe, again in the space between the tomb and a surrounding ditch. All that survived of the tomb itself was a beautifully constructed entrance-passage, the quality of which suggests that the chamber would have

43 *Maes Howe: the main chamber and a side-cell.*

been a delight to behold.

The interior design of Maes Howe is symmetrical and precise, spacious and elegant. Despite its scale, the height of the passage means that entry can only be gained by stooping low (**42**); not only does this reinforce the impression that a show of respect was required of those wishing to enter, but it also intensifies the impact on the senses of the lofty chamber. Reaching it, there is suddenly great space, the effect of which would be magnified in the dark or half-light, subterranean chill and an intense stillness.

Huge slabs of stone were used in the passage, as paving stones, as side-slabs and as roofing (see **9**). The tomb could be sealed by a massive triangular block, which now occupies the recess built to house it, when not in use, in the left-hand side of the passage. The block would fill the width of the passage, but additional stones would have to be placed on top in order to close the gap between the block and the roof.

The passage opens into a square chamber, fully 4.7m (13ft) across, and in the centre of each of the other three walls and some 0.8m (2ft 8in) above the floor is the entrance to a side-cell (**43**). Large blocks of stone now on the floor of the chamber are likely to have been used to seal the cells. The chamber is roofed by a square vault, strengthened by a buttress in each corner, and the technical artistry of the masonry is superb. A meticulous attention to detail can be seen in the way in which the walls gradually oversail, slabs underpinned where necessary by flakes of stone, and in the way in which the surfaces of large blocks have been dressed flush with the wall. The apex of the roof is modern, but the original height may have been 4.5m (15ft) high or more.

The only original decoration in the chamber is a lightly incised design which was recorded in the last century but recognized as Neolithic only recently by Patrick Ashmore (see **49** F). It seems oddly inconsequential against the grandeur of the architecture.

The most tantalizing aspect of Maes Howe is that nothing is known about how the chamber and cells were used. A single fragment of human skull was found amongst debris in one of the cells in the nineteenth-century excavation. The many runic inscriptions on the walls of the chamber imply that it was empty of filling when Norsemen broke into the mound in the twelfth century, and none of the inscriptions mentions bones. Several mention treasure, but if a treasure, which to Norsemen would mean gold or silver, had truly been found in the tomb, it could only imply that the tomb had been re-used for a later burial. Gold was in use in the British Isles for prestigious jewellery by the middle of the second millennium BC, and some was acquired by Orcadian potentates (see p.89). One argument in favour of re-use a few centuries after its construction might be based on the fact that, in overall appearance, Maes Howe looks very much like an oversized disc barrow, a type of burial monument used in the Bronze Age. At least two such disc barrows were built in the Loch of Harray area (p.91).

Silverwork belongs to much later times and in Orkney makes its first appearance in the early centuries AD, becoming plentiful in the Viking period, when gold was also coveted. The sequence of radiocarbon dates associated with the ditch and bank indicate that the bank was rebuilt in the Viking period in the ninth century AD. Why? The most economical way to explain both the rebuilding and the inscribed references to treasure is to propose that Maes Howe was re-used for the burial of a Viking warlord and his treasure in the ninth century, only to be ransacked by his own descendants in the twelfth.

Either explanation would also account for the emptiness of the tomb, for the remaining Neolithic burials would have been removed in order to make it ready for the important new occupant. It is also possible that the tomb was already empty.

The Maes Howe-type tomb at Quanterness was not filled with earth and stones as a final process of sealing the chamber, and neither, it would appear, was Maes Howe itself. The only tomb of this type known definitely to have been sealed in this way is Wideford Hill. When George Petrie opened the chamber in the mid-nineteenth century, he found it virtually filled with earth and stones which had clearly been poured in from a hole in the roof. Despite this deliberate closure of the tomb, no trace of human burials was found within it, whereas Quanterness retained a mass of human bones. Such differences emphasize the wide range of ritual activities encompassed by chambered tombs.

Quanterness

The tomb at Quanterness lies on the lower northern flank of Wideford Hill, well below and to the north-east of the smaller tomb named after the hill. Quanterness was first opened at the beginning of the nineteenth century, but its contents appeared not to have been removed, and this encouraged Colin Renfrew to mount an excavation in 1972. Within its round cairn, the tomb consists of an entrance passage opening into one long side of a rectangular chamber. Six side-cells are arranged symmetrically round the chamber, one at each end and two opening off each of the long sides. A curious feature not encountered elsewhere is a small 'window' opening into one of the cells from the main chamber; this may have played a part in the ceremonies that took place within the tomb. On the floor of the chamber was a thick layer of human bones mixed with animal, bird and fish bones, stones and soil. Before this deposit had begun to accumulate, fires had been lit on the floor and three burial pits had been dug through the floor. The bone layer extended into the cells and into the entrance passage. One of the very latest burials was represented by a skeleton in a shallow pit scooped into the top of the bone layer, opposite the entrance into the tomb. Renfrew decided that a large sample of the contents of the tomb should be left intact for study by future archaeologists, and he excavated only one of the cells and some 80% of the main chamber.

The excavated deposits yielded the remains of 157 people. If the unexcavated areas contain a similar density of bones, it is likely that some 400 individuals were buried in the tomb. Artefacts were scattered throughout the bone layer, including sherds from at least 34 Grooved Ware vessels and a wide variety of domestic equipment from hammerstones and bone pins to flint knives and an antler hammer.

Quoyness

Quanterness was sealed after the excavation, but a good impression of its interior can be gained by a visit to Quoyness in Sanday. This tomb lies close to the shore on a long flat promontory, known as Elsness, which today is barely above the level of high tide but which was used for some 26 burial-cairns, probably of Bronze Age date. The external appearance of this tomb is somewhat misleading. After excavation by Gordon Childe in the early 1950s, the cairn was reconstructed to show the stages by which it had been built rather than its final form. The design of the chamber and six cells is very similar to that at Quanterness, and there are two pits dug into the clay floor (44).

The tomb had first been opened by James Farrer in 1867, and, as at Holm of Papa Westray North, he left most of the human bones in the chamber. They represented the remains of about 15 people who had been buried in the main chamber, in four of the six side-cells and in the entrance passage. These are likely to be only the best-preserved bones, however, and the original total of burials may have been higher. The few

artefacts from the chamber and cells include special items that would not be out of place at Skara Brae: two curious spiked objects carefully made of slate (see 51) and a large bone pin with a knob on the shank.

Orientation of passages

The passage of Maes Howe faces south-west, and the setting sun at midwinter shines along the passage and into the chamber, illuminating the rear wall. Aubrey Burl has suggested that the reason why the great blocking stone does not fill the height of the passage may be that the gap was deliberately designed to allow the sun's rays to penetrate the tomb. Most Orcadian chambered tombs were built in such a position, however, that the entrance passage faced between east-north-east and south. This is likely to have had some general connection with the midwinter

44 *Inside Quoyness, the entrances to the cells are dwarfed by the height of the main chamber; a pit is visible in the floor between the end-cell and the cell on the left.*

sunrise in the south-east, the time of year at which the brief winter days begin to lengthen and the hope of spring grows stronger. But there may well have been other local factors that also influenced this orientation. It was presumably local factors that governed the exceptions to this general orientation. The passage at Holm of Papa Westray North faces north-west, partly perhaps because the primary cell was thus oriented and partly because that was the direction of access along the contemporary promontory. The later tomb at the south end of the Holm was oriented towards the normal south-east quadrant.

Ancestors

Fundamental to the design of all chambered tombs was the idea that it should be possible to go in and out of the chamber at will rather than on a single occasion. In this respect, the tomb resembles the family burial vault of more recent times, but there is an important difference. Whereas the burial vault was intended to hold individual members of the family whose remains were respected as individuals throughout time, chambered tombs appear to have housed members of the community who may have been buried singly but whose individuality was not considered important. Their bones were mixed together, sorted into piles of long bones and separate skulls and moved about to suit the purposes of the living community.

All ages of people and both sexes were considered appropriate for burial in the tombs. There is no obvious trace of élitism, and no reason not to assume that most people in the community were given formal burial in this way. The two women buried beneath one of the houses at Skara Brae show that not everyone ended up in a chambered tomb, but such burials appear to have been rare. The two largest bone assemblages excavated in modern times are those from Isbister and Quanterness, and both tell the same story. To quote only the figures from Quanterness, there were 85 adults, 36

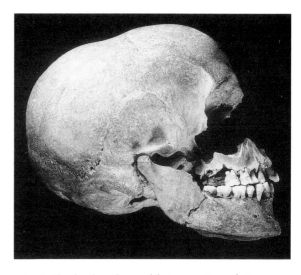

45 *Skull of a female aged between 25 and 30 years from Isbister; note the depression in the forehead which is thought to be the result of carrying heavy loads on the back supported by a band round the head.*

teenagers, 26 children between the ages of 2 and 12, and 10 infants between the ages of 8 months and 2 years. The average life expectancy at 8 months was 20–25 years, and adults could expect to develop osteoarthritis, particularly of the spine (**45**). Adult height was on average two or three centimetres (1in) less than that of the modern population. Very few people, only 11 out of the 85 adults, lived beyond their twenties, and the eldest was about 50 years. The older people in such a predominantly young population would have been vitally important in handing on knowledge and experience.

If only to keep out predatory animals, it would be necessary to seal the tomb between visits. At Maes Howe, the passage was clearly sealed by the great block of stone still housed there in 'open' position, and the Dwarfie Stane was sealed in the same way by the block now lying outside. (This rock-cut tomb in Hoy is discussed in chapter 9.) Elsewhere there is evidence to show that the entrance was closed with drystone walling, which could be taken down and rebuilt as required (**46**). Another device might be to wedge in place a single flagstone. At the inner

46 *The entrance into the tomb at Midhowe was blocked in two places by masonry.*

end of the passage at Holm of Papa Westray North was such a slab, lying flat when excavated but it could have been wedged against the portal stones.

There appear to be enormous contrasts between the numbers of people buried in the tombs, from a dozen or so to several hundred. But there are also other factors to be considered. Foremost is the situation at the point of final closure, for the state of the tomb when excavated reflects only its final circumstances. Nothing can be known of how many times the tomb may have been cleared out during the period of its use, or of how many bones may have been removed for whatever purpose. Natural decay and intrusion into the tomb by animals and birds must be taken into consideration, for they affect the contents of the chamber both during its use and for many centuries afterwards. Some tombs were apparently empty when sealed, implying that

total clearance could be part of the activities involved in their use.

Skeletons are very rarely, if ever, complete and they may be represented by a few bones or many bones. This fact has led several archaeologists to argue that excarnation was practised the custom known from anthropological studies whereby a body is left to become defleshed before the bones are gathered up and buried. Defleshing can be achieved in several ways; one is to expose the body on a platform to the air and to carrion-eating birds such as vultures and eagles. Another method is to bury the body in a temporary grave until only the bones are left. In either case, the completeness of the skeleton will depend upon the care with which the bones are collected and placed in the tomb. Excarnation was put forward to explain the marked losses among the bones surviving at both Quanterness and Isbister. For example, at Isbister, there were only 39 carpals from the wrists of 185 adults each of whom ought to have had 16, and although the spines of that number of people ought to have been represented by some 3000 vertebrae, there were in fact only about 158 mostly from the top of the spine.

Nevertheless, most archaeologists believe that there is insufficient evidence to support the idea that excarnation was practised regularly in Neolithic Orkney.

The missing bones may never have been taken into the tomb, but equally they may have been removed from the tomb subsequent to burial. Small bones may have disappeared through natural decay. There were skeletons in a crouched position at Midhowe and elsewhere, which can only represent complete bodies placed in the tomb, as well as piles of mixed bones from partial skeletons. It is logical to assume that, when new burials were made, or indeed on other occasions, older skeletons were gathered up or pushed to one side. In some cases the bones were sorted, leading at the Knowe of Yarso to the arrangement of skulls alone in the innermost compartment.

There could be many reasons for removing

bones from a tomb. If the presence of ancestors had a territorial significance, in the sense of justifying a community's claim to its land, bones might be taken elsewhere to justify territorial expansion or change of ownership. Ancestral bones might be needed for ceremonies elsewhere, in which case a finger-bone found in the ditch at the Stones of Stenness might have some significance. A skull lay in the forecourt in front of the entrance to Holm of Papa Westray North, and bones of a child were found in the filling of the entrance-passage; neither are likely to have been accidental, and they may have been removed from this tomb or another tomb in order to use them in this way. The filling of the chamber at Isbister included deliberate deposits of human bone. It seems that the question of whether or not excarnation was practised must remain open. Straightforward inhumation was certainly practised, and it was probably the normal and dominant rite.

Ritual within the tomb

A number of tombs have yielded evidence of ritual activities within the chamber, apart from those involved in the placing of bodies and the re-arrangement of bones. There were clearly rules to be followed, even though the rules might vary over time and between communities. Fire played a role in some ceremonies, leaving burnt patches on chamber floors and occasionally on walls, as well as scorched bones and artefacts. Some rules concerned the use of space within the chamber (**47**). One side of the chamber might be designated for burials, as at Midhowe, and one area for artefacts, as at Isbister where a huge amount of broken pottery was concentrated in a mound along the wall opposite the entrance. Other rules governed the closure of parts of the chamber and the final sealing of the entire tomb. The selection of material considered appropriate to the closure of the cell at Holm of Papa Westray North has already been discussed; similar care went into filling the entrance passage in three sections along its length, the middle

section consisting of densely packed limpet shells and fishbones. The filling of the chamber itself was laced with deer tines.

Remains of animals, birds and fish have been found among the floor deposits in tombs excavated in modern times, and it is likely that in older excavations they were simply not regarded as important or, in the case of fish, not noticed. An element of natural intrusion may account for some of the smaller bones of rodents and fish, for otters and owls have certainly penetrated into some tombs, and, if the passage were inadequately blocked, larger animals such as young sheep could wriggle in as well. After excavating the tomb at Point of Cott in Westray, John Barber argued that most, if not all, of the non-human bones had arrived by natural means. Elsewhere, however, the bulk of the organic remains seems to have taken into the chambers by their users. Some, especially fishbones, are likely to have arrived in the deposits of soil from domestic middens which were placed in the chambers, but much represents deliberate inclusion of food with burials. Joints of mutton and beef were taken into Quanterness, along with parts of very young lambs and an unusual variety of small birds. There was also an emphasis upon young animals at Isbister, whereas parts of at least 30 sheep of all ages lay on the floor at Holm of Papa Westray North. A heap of limpets was left in the first compartment in Midhowe. All this sounds like food offerings, but there are also instances of curious concentrations of one particular species, which raise the possibility of some form of totemism.

The bodies of seven dogs were left in the chamber at Burray, and a heap of 24 dog-skulls at Cuween. Within a small stone box in the innermost compartment at Holm of Papa Westray North were 9kg (20lb) of very small fishbones. Deer tines were common at Holm, and bones at Knowe of Yarso and Knowe of Ramsay represented respectively 36 and 14 red deer. Isbister earned its nickname, Tomb of the Eagles, because there were bones and talons of white-tailed sea-eagles both on the floor and in

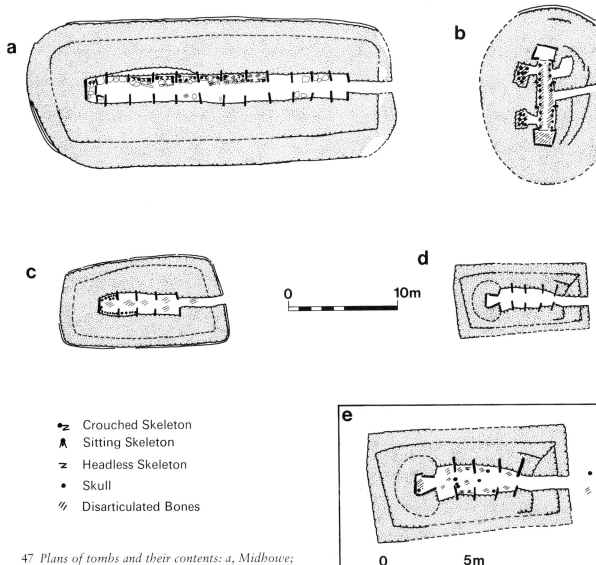

47 *Plans of tombs and their contents: a, Midhowe; b, Isbister (schematic); c, Yarso; d and e, Holm of Papa Westray North.*

the filling of the chamber. This is a magnificent bird with a wingspan of almost 2m (6.5ft) and a lifespan longer than most of its human companions in the tomb. It may well be that Neolithic communities identified themselves with a particular animal or bird, although the only supporting evidence from a settlement are the deer skeletons at Links of Noltland (p.38). Perhaps even more likely is that these special deposits represent a need to seek supernatural help to maintain or increase the stocks of animals and fish upon which life depended. But again a note of caution is needed. At Point of Cott, the innermost compartment of the stalled chamber contained 36 talons of a large bird of prey, along with many other bird bones, which John Barber has interpreted as a bird population resident in the tomb.

1 (*Above*) A house complete with stone furniture at Skara Brae.

2 (*Right*) Inside the chambered tomb at Cuween.

3   (*Below*) The chambered tomb at Wideford overlooks the Bay of Firth.

4   (*Top right*) The low entrance to an end-cell at Holm of Papa Westray South makes survey difficult.

5   (*Bottom right*) The Ring of Brodgar from the air.

6   (*Overleaf, left*) The Stones of Stenness.

7   (*Overleaf, right*) Gold button-covers from a burial at Knowes of Trotty.

8   (*Above*) The broch of
    Gurness.

9   (*Left*) The broch of
    Midhowe and the west end
    of Eynhallow Sound.

10 (*Right*) Inside the broch of
    Midhowe.

11   The earth-house at Grain.

The lifespan of chambered tombs

With radiocarbon dates from eight Orcadian tombs (five stalled cairns and three Maes Howe-type), it is clear that the lifespan of a tomb may have been half a millennium or more. Both stalled cairns and Maes Howe-type tombs appear to have been in existence before 3000 BC, as one would expect from the dating of related settlements, and it seems possible that the main period of tomb-building was over soon after that date. Some remained in use at least until about 2500. The earliest radiocarbon dates come from Quanterness, but overall it is likely that some stalled cairns were in use at an earlier date than the construction of Maes Howe-type tombs, mirroring the evidence from settlements that Unstan Ware was in use somewhat earlier than Grooved Ware. This impression is supported by the fact that Grooved Ware pottery and artefacts have been found outside stalled cairns and associated with the final closure of stalled cairns, but never as part of the primary use of the tomb. There is no good dating evidence from the tripartite tombs which were probably the first type of tomb to be built in Orkney.

Estimates of labour

As Audrey Henshall has written of chambered tombs, 'The effort expended on them during the brief pain-ridden lives of their builders is remarkable'. The number of people buried in a tomb has no relation to the size of the tomb, but the size of the tomb has a direct bearing on the labour needed to build it. Their tombs were a far greater enterprise in terms of labour than their houses and were only to be exceeded by the great ceremonial circles. It is difficult to estimate the number of people who might have been available to help in building a tomb, because there are so many unknown factors. Colin Renfrew suggested that Quanterness may have contained all the dead from a group of around 20 individuals over a period of about 550 years; this estimate assumes that the bones in the tomb at the time of closure are an accurate reflection of those buried there, but, as discussed already, bones may have been removed or added. It is also possible that an extended family group intending to build a tomb may have been able to call upon the help of other such groups, particularly as some of the group will have been either too young or too infirm to help.

The most useful way to approach the question of the labour involved in the building process is to estimate the number of man-hours required. Thus, if the construction of a small tomb would require some 1000 man-hours of labour, it could have been accomplished by ten people each putting in 100 hours or forty people each working 25 hours. How many hours a day they might work is, of course, another imponderable factor! In estimating the man-hours required to build Quanterness, Colin Renfrew used figures available for traditional methods of quarrying stone and drystone building in Orkney, and he arrived at a minimum total of 10,000 man-hours. This would have been an enormous task for a small community, however they solved the problem of labour. Larger tombs such as Holm of Papa Westray South might have required some 15,000 man-hours, while the labour for Maes Howe, with its huge slabs that had to be transported some distance from the quarry, probably needed closer to 100,000 man-hours. Such extravagant expenditure of human effort carries implications for social and economic development, which will be discussed in chapter 5, alongside the other ceremonial monuments that were raised early in the third millennium BC.

CHAPTER FOUR

The role of art in life and death

A magnificent carved stone was discovered during quarrying in Westray in January 1981. The superb quality of the carving and its excellent preservation make this the most important example of prehistoric art in Scotland (**48**). The quarry lies on the links behind the Bay of Pierowall at the north end of the island, and the quarry-face at that time had exposed the edge of a low mound. A rescue excavation was mounted by Niall Sharples, who interpreted the site as a Maes Howe-type chambered tomb within a circular cairn; the tomb had been demolished around 3000 BC and the area paved over to form a flint-working platform. Some 2000 years later, a round-house was built on the low mound of debris that hid the earlier structures (p.96).

The flint-working was associated with Grooved Ware, and thus the deliberate destruction of the tomb appears to have been carried out by people belonging to the same social and cultural group as those who built the tomb in the first place. In a sense this destruction could be seen as equivalent to the final closure and infilling that took place at other tombs, but it was undeniably more dramatic and labour-intensive. The bones of the ancestors may been removed prior to the destruction and taken elsewhere (some human bones were found outside the cairn). Even so, the act seems inexplicable. Moreover, compared with other tombs, Pierowall's period of use was over very early. There may, of course, be other demolished tombs, traces of which have simply not been found or not recognized; without the distinctive stone-carving at Pierowall, it is doubtful whether the site would have been recognized as a

48 *Carved stone from Pierowall.*

chambered cairn. It was built on the 20m (66ft) OD contour, only about half a mile from the Grooved Ware settlement at Links of Noltland, where occupation began at broadly the same time that Pierowall was destroyed. Could these two events have been linked in some way?

It is, however, only the size of the cairn, estimated from the surviving arc to have been 18m (59ft) in diameter, and the stone-carving that imply the presence of a Maes Howe-type tomb. Otherwise it would be possible to argue for an earlier type of tomb, demolished by a rival social group and the site converted into a workshop making flint artefacts and decorated stones.

If this was indeed the site of a Maes Howe-type cairn, the high quality of the carving may suggest that the tomb itself was architecturally impressive, but too little survived even of the demolished basal courses to judge. The stone is thought to have come from the area of the entrance, and to have been a lintel visible from outside. Two other decorated stones were found amongst the quarry-spoil, but these are of lesser quality and nothing is known about their original position in the cairn. All three bear similar motifs consisting of linked spirals, which were created first by pecking and, in the case of the 'lintel', smoothed into V-section grooves.

Pierowall is not alone in Orkney in yielding carved stones. Very similar motifs decorate a slab from a tomb of Maes Howe type in Eday (49H), which was largely destroyed in 1821 to build a church. The Neolithic tomb had survived almost 5000 years, but the church is already in ruins. From old records, it seems that the decorated slab was probably a lintel over the entrance into one of a large number of side-cells. Such a lintel is still in position in the tomb at the south end of Holm of Papa Westray (49I), where there are also a number of other decorated slabs in the walls of the main chamber. Here the decoration is far less formal and required far less skill. Closer in style to the stones from Westray and Eday is a slab found in a mound at Pickaquoy on the south-west flank of Wideford Hill (49G). Its findspot is a burnt mound, likely

to belong to the end of the second or early first millennium BC (p.95), but the stone was probably re-used, and it may imply the presence nearby of a destroyed Maes Howe-type tomb.

All the known examples of Neolithic architectural art (apart from cup-and-ring carvings) in Scotland come from Orkney, and there are clear links with contemporary art in Ireland. The 'lintel' stone from Pierowall, in particular, would look very much at home embellishing one of the superbly decorated tombs in the Boyne valley north of Dublin. More difficult to estimate is just how the link between Ireland and Orkney manifested itself in human terms, and whether it was a direct link. As Audrey Henshall has pointed out, 'The loss of art in perishable media is likely to endow the rare examples which have survived with exceptionally distorted significance and values'.

Curvilinear motifs and dots appear to have been the accepted norm for the decoration of Maes Howe-type tombs, although at Maes Howe itself the only Neolithic decoration is linear and closer in its graffito style of light incision to the art of the settlements (49F). But this is not an immutable distinction, for the stone from Pool has linear decoration which is pecked rather than incised (49L). No chambered cairn of the stalled or related forms has yet produced any architectural art, nor are the houses at Knap of Howar decorated. No ornament was noticed on the buildings at Rinyo, but two factors could account for its absence here: only the basal wall-courses survived and only a small part of the site was excavated. By analogy with Skara Brae, decoration could have been confined to a part of the settlement that was not uncovered.

There is a remarkable number of decorated stones from Skara Brae, both built into the standing walls and found loose in the midden. The most elaborate are illustrated here (49B–E; 50), and the motifs are mostly based on chevrons, triangles and zig-zag, executed by incised lines or occasionally by pecking. Very simple tools would produce the desired effect on these relatively soft slabs; flint blades were

49 *Art motifs of the fourth and third millennium:*
A, Skara Brae potsherd; B–E, Skara Brae stones;
F, Maes Howe stone; G, Pickaquoy stone; H, Eday
Manse stone; I, Holm of Papa Westray South
stone; J, Ness of Brodgar stone; K, Barnhouse
stone; L, Pool stone. (not to scale)

50 *Decorated stone in the wall of house 8 at Skara Brae.*

probably used for incised design, and flint or flaked stone chisels and hammerstones for pecked motifs.

The same art style appears at the Barnhouse settlement (**49K**), and, more formally, on the narrow face of a slab found not far away on the Ness of Brodgar (**49J**). This last stone was discovered partially covering two large cists, and, because these are likely to have been of Bronze Age date and because the decoration on the stone was reminiscent of that on beaker pottery of similar date, the stone was thought also to belong to the Bronze Age. Now, however, the repertoire of Neolithic art has widened to include more such linear designs, and in particular decoration in bands echoing in less formal style the bands on the Brodgar stone. The stone is triangular and looks more like a building-slab than a cist-cover. It seems possible that it may have been taken from the settlement at Barnhouse and re-used in the Brodgar cemetery.

Many of the decorated stones at Skara Brae have a casual appearance, and it is difficult to know how much symbolism can justifiably be

attributed to the designs themselves and to the location of the stones within the settlement. It was suggested earlier (p.34) that their overall distribution may have a chronological significance, for they belong to the most developed stage of the evolution of the settlement. Most of the decoration was carved on passage walls, and only two houses, 7 and 8, were decorated internally. These two houses appear to have fulfilled functions that were different from 'normal' domestic houses (p.34), and the ornament may have had a special significance in these contexts. In most cases the decoration was placed at a low height. Although attempts have been made to find significant patterns in the position of the stones, there is no clear preference for left or right, or around doorways, on walls or on furniture. If decoration carried special meaning other than a pleasure in its existence, the key is hidden.

Even the apparent distinction between curvilinear designs in tombs and geometric designs in the home is blurred by the decoration on portable artefacts. The Grooved Ware from the tomb at Quanterness bears linear decoration, while that from settlements tends towards curvilinear decoration, often in relief. A sherd from

Skara Brae has become the best-known piece of Neolithic pottery in Scotland. The design has been reconstructed as a symmetrical motif consisting of two spirals and two lozenges (see **49A**), and it has been adopted by modern artists and made, for example, into silver brooches and cuff-links. Some doubt has been cast on the accuracy of the reconstruction, but it will no doubt continue to act as Skara Brae's logo.

Simple linear decoration occurs on a wide range of artefacts from Skara Brae, but elsewhere portable decoration is confined to pottery. Perhaps the shape of objects may also be seen as decorative, particularly the curious stone objects from Quoyness (**51**). There may have been a whole range of decorated wooden and leather items that has not survived. It may be significant that personal adornment was part of the Skara Brae life-style, in the form of necklaces of bone

and ivory beads and pendants, and large bone pins which may have acted either as dress-fasteners or as hair ornaments. Body-painting is also possible; red ochre was ground in small bone and stone vessels, and the powder was mixed with fat to make a soft paste. A small ball of this paste was found inside a pot made from a whale's vertebra. Paint may have illuminated some of the carved stones or decorated skin garments.

Even commonplace tools such as flaked stone knives ('Skaill knives') were sometimes decorated; one has triangles filled with lozenges incised on its rounded surface, and another has bands of zig-zag and lozenges (**52**). But there are several ornamental stone objects from Skara Brae, the purpose of which is far from obvious and which are therefore assumed to be ceremonial. Amongst them are two balls, one 62mm (2½in) in diameter and incised with geometric decoration, and the other 77mm (3in) in diameter and painstakingly carved into knobs and

51 *Carved stone objects from Quoyness.*

52 *A decorated 'Skaill knife' from Skara Brae.*

grooves. There is also an oval ball, 92mm (3½in) long, with four knobs at either end and panels of grooves in a band round the middle, and a spiked or T-shaped object with a central band of incised decoration, again in panels (53). These two objects are very similar to those from Quoyness, though more highly decorated, and they appear to be unique to Orkney. Whatever the concept that lay behind the carved stone balls, they were widespread beyond Orkney. Almost 400 have been found, mostly in north-east Scotland between the River Tay and the Moray Firth, although examples have also been found in the far west. Some of the balls from north-east Scotland bear very elaborate and finely carved ornament. Although few have been found in datable contexts, they are normally assigned to the third and second millennia BC.

Some doubt has been cast recently on the date of some of the carved stone balls by James Macaulay, an engineer who has carried out practical experiments in making such balls. In some cases the angle created in the decoration of prehistoric balls has proved impossible to achieve with stone tools and can only have been carved with strong metal tools. Macaulay feels that, while some balls were made and used in Neolithic times, others may have been reworked

or made entirely at a later period, particularly in Pictish times when similar decorative designs were fashionable. His experiments have also proved illuminating about the effort and time that went into the creation of a carved stone ball, from the initial choice of a suitable pebble to the finished product; producing a sandstone sphere 63mm (2½in) in diameter with stone tools took only three hours (and an experienced stone-worker might take less), whereas the decoration was far more time consuming. A ball with simple decoration could be made in a morning, but carving an elaborately decorated ball might take three days. Sandstone is relatively soft, and harder stones such as granite take longer to shape. The T-shaped object from Skara Brae was made from a very hard stone by pecking and grinding, and Gordon Childe described it as 'one of the most astounding monuments of human skill and patience known'.

Stone balls and T-shaped objects seem best interpreted as symbols of status and prestige, akin to ceremonial regalia still in use in the modern world. A ball might be passed round a gathering of people, conveying upon the holder the right to speak, or a number of sacred objects

53 *Some of the enigmatic stone objects from Skara Brae.*

might be carried in procession. A person of special rank might be marked out by possession of one of these objects. Stone maceheads are likely to have acted in a similar way, for they are finely made, often from particularly attractive rocks, and show little trace of practical use (**54**). These were presumably mounted on wooden hafts. One from Skara Brae is carved, like many stone balls, into multiple knobs, and the perforation has such an exaggerated hour-glass shape that it was probably not mounted on a handle. No fewer than 76 maceheads have been found in Orkney, mostly made of stone but also made of antler and whalebone. This figure marks a higher concentration of maceheads here than anywhere else in Britain or Ireland. Most were found in Mainland, but a significant number has been found in the larger islands, except Hoy (where there is little evidence for settlement at this period) and, more surprisingly, Eday. Ten come from the Brodgar-Stenness area of central Mainland, where there is structural evidence of ceremonial activities (see chapter 5). Many maceheads are stray finds with no archaeological context, but they have also been found in settlements and tombs.

The high incidence of maceheads in Orkney underlines the importance of ceremony and prestige to Orcadian communities of the fourth and third millennia. Ideas and beliefs are very difficult to define from material remains, but plenty of clues have been noted in the last two chapters to show that ritual was involved in both life and death, even if the precise nature of that ritual is elusive. It was expressed in the architecture of houses and tombs and, we assume, in the use of art.

Anthropological studies of primitive societies of the nineteenth and twentieth centuries are a useful source of information about ways in which archaeological material may be interpreted. Closer to home, the rich folklore of the Northern Isles and Highlands of Scotland can be invaluable in suggesting some of the areas in which there may have been customary practices that would leave little or no trace in the

54 *Stone maceheads.*

archaeological record. For example, in Westray, the grain from the very first barley to be harvested was threshed, dried, ground and used for a ritual meal, normally eaten by the head of the household. Nothing of this custom could be gleaned from physical traces in the ground. All sorts of unlucky circumstances could affect fishing. Limpets for bait were knocked off the rocks with a thin piece of stone; when the pail was full, the fisherman would fling the stone away with as much force as he could muster. If it shattered, he would have good fishing, but, if it remained intact, he might just as well stay at home. There were rituals surrounding many areas of everyday life. Building a house in Shetland meant ensuring that there was an 'earth-fast stane', a stone firmly embedded in the earth which was part of the basal course of the house-wall. In Orkney, a handful of 'holy stones', small white quartz pebbles, or a flint knife was hidden somewhere in the walls. Many traditions surrounded the major landmarks of human life, such as birth, marriage and death, and the series of formal ritual activities surrounding marriage, in particular, lend a flavour of the past. Marriage, after all, is a social contract.

CHAPTER FIVE

Tribal organization and ceremony

The spiritual node of Orkney 5000 years ago lay in a place where water, land and sky had a special interwoven relationship. In Mainland, the two great lochs of Stenness and Harray are stretched out alongside one another, Stenness to the west and Harray to the east. Today they are both freshwater lochs, although salt water finds its way into the Loch of Stenness at the Bridge of Waithe from the sea in the Bay of Ireland. It is likely that, in Neolithic times when sea-level was higher, the water in the loch was mostly if not totally saline. The two lochs would then represent not only west and east, sunset and sunrise, but also saltwater and freshwater, with all that those two liquids imply for human life.

At their closest point, the two lochs are separated by the narrow neck of land known as the Ness of Brodgar, and an artificial causeway links the tip of the Ness with the Stenness peninsula. A map drawn for Sir Joseph Banks in 1772 shows the gap between the two promontories to have been narrower then, and it is possible that there was no gap five millennia ago.

There was thus a special relationship between the two lochs. They are surrounded by low hills, which give the impression of a huge shallow bowl, and yet the bowl is wide open to the sky. It is also open to the south-west to the higher hills of Hoy, almost 500m (1640 ft) above sea-level at the summit of Ward Hill, and these hills constitute an important skyline for the monuments within the bowl.

Ritual and burial monuments are thick on the ground between the two lochs, to the extent that it is legitimate to regard the Brodgar-Stenness area as Orkney's ceremonial centre (55). The idea of such a focal area is not unique to Orkney, for others have been identified in Scotland at Callanish in Lewis, the Kilmartin Valley in Argyll and Balfarg in Fife. Nor is it unique to prehistory, for many places have become specially important to spiritual life in later times, for instance Iona in Argyll and Glastonbury in Somerset.

The earliest surviving monument in the Brodgar-Stenness area is likely to be the small chambered cairn at Bookan, to the north-west of the Ring of Brodgar. There is a stalled cairn at Unstan, overlooking the entry into the Loch of Stenness from the sea, but this is not likely to have been an early example. To the north-west of Bookan is the Ring of Bookan, an earthen circle which is thought to have been a ceremonial site; the space enclosed is similar in size to that inside the ditch at the Stones of Stenness. Such earthwork circles, normally consisting of a ditch with an external bank as at Stenness, are known as henges, and they are a type of ceremonial monument that is common throughout Britain and unique to Britain. The date of the Ring of Bookan is unknown, but the Stones of Stenness, where the earthwork henge was embellished by a circle of standing stones, has radiocarbon dates which imply that it was in existence by 3000 BC.

The next monuments to be built were the tomb at Maes Howe and the larger henge and

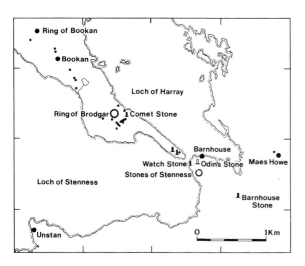

55 Map of the ceremonial centre of Orkney between the Lochs of Harray and Stenness.

stone circle known as the Ring of Brodgar, perhaps around the middle of the third millennium. Towards the end of the millennium a wide range of burial mounds began to be built. The various isolated standing stones are impossible to date closely, but the Watch Stone in particular may have been an outlier of the Stenness circle and erected early in the millennium. The area remained an active focus for ceremonies and burials during the second millennium, and its fame and mystery outlived pagan times (p.119).

The Stones of Stenness

In the early 1970s, Graham Ritchie conducted a research excavation at the Stones of Stenness, with the aim of answering a number of important questions about the original form of the monument. It had had an unusually chequered history over the previous two centuries. Old records and drawings show that, in the eighteenth century, there were four standing stones and the stump of a fifth, a large slab lying on the ground almost in the centre of the circle, and an encircling bank. When Sir Walter Scott visited the site in August 1814, he thought that the

horizontal slab was 'probably once the altar on which human victims were sacrificed'. Less than four months later, disaster struck the monument. The farmer lost patience with the problems of ploughing round the stones, and began to demolish them. Prompt local action forced him to give up his plan (p.11), but not before he had destroyed one stone and toppled another.

The circle remained in this condition until 1906 when it was taken into State care. The toppled stone was then re-erected, and another stone was discovered lying beneath the turf and subsequently placed upright in an existing socket-hole. This was the angled stone, now no. 7. Local opinion had its doubts about this 'ill-shaped' stone: 'It looks such a dwarf amid these huge monoliths'. Even today most artistic photographs contrive to omit it, or to show it sideways (**56**), but it is visible in the photograph taken in 1907 (see **91**). It looks out of place to us, but it may well have had a special significance to the builders of the circle. In 1907, the horizontal slab that Sir Walter Scott had taken to be part of an altar was raised as just that, the top of a table-like structure.

But sometimes mistakes have a way of rectifying themselves. One night in October 1972, some 65 years later, the table-top was pushed off – the victim of a drunken party it was said, but who knows? The problem now was whether or not to reconstruct the 'altar'. This is where Graham Ritchie and his team came into the story. Their task was to excavate round the 'altar' to find out whether there was any genuine evidence for such a structure, and to discover more about the circle and its ditch and bank, by now ploughed flat. The first step was to have the area surveyed with scientific instruments which detect any buried anomalies, for these would be evidence of places where the ground has been disturbed in the past. This geophysical survey showed clearly the position of the ditch and a gap on the north side which must be an entrance; it also showed that there was some sort of central structure and a number of pits of varying sizes.

56 (Above) *The Stones of Stenness with the hills of Hoy in the distance.*

57 (Below) *Plan of the Stones of Stenness as excavated in the 1970s.*

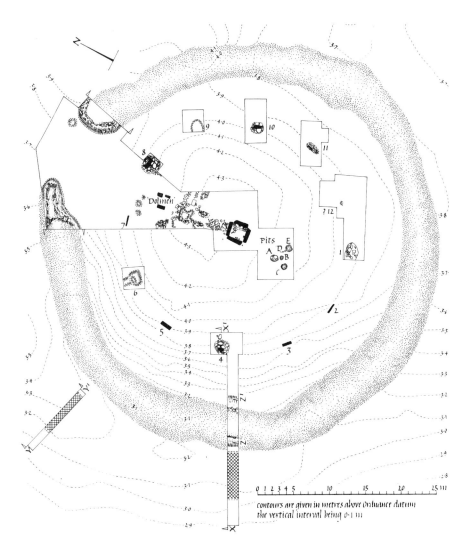

contours are given in metres above Ordnance datum
the vertical interval being 0·1 m

58 (Above) *Stones of Stenness: excavation under difficult conditions of one of the ditch-ends.*

stones within a circular area about 44m (144ft) in diameter. The sequence of construction is unknown, but economy of effort would demand that the standing stones should be raised before the ditch was dug and the bank piled up. It would otherwise be very difficult to work in such a confined space.

Originally there were twelve stones in a circle about 30m across. If all the stones were as tall as those that survive – no. 2 is 5.7m (19ft) high – this must have been a most impressive sight; the height of the uprights would have accentuated the compact diameter of the circle. Although only four stones can be seen today, the holes for the stones and in some cases the stumps of the stones were found for the other members of the circle (**59**).

What, if anything, lay at the centre of a circle like this? Excavation uncovered a square setting

The plan shows the ditch and where trenches were excavated to reveal buried features (**57**). Outside the ditch were traces of a bank, making this a typical example of a henge monument. The ditch itself was 7m (23ft) wide at the top and about 2.3m (7½ft) deep with a flat bottom, and the lower part proved to have been cut into the solid bedrock (**58**). The rock must have been prised out laboriously with wedges and picks. The bottom of the ditch was below the water-table, and the water had to be pumped out continuously during the excavation. While the ditch was open, during the use of the site, some interesting organic material had been thrown into it. There were bones of cattle and sheep, mostly from parts of the animal least likely to have been eaten, such as feet, together with dog bones and a human finger-bone. Cattle and sheep may have been slaughtered for sacrifice or feasting or both. The damp ditch-deposits also contained plant remains, which show that the monument was constructed in an area of open grassland and that there was some cereal cultivation in the vicinity.

The bank and ditch enclosed a ring of standing

59 (Below) *Stones of Stenness: excavation of stump of stone 8, showing stone packing around its base.*

60 *Artist's reconstruction of a ceremony at the Stones of Stenness, with the Ring of Brodgar and other standing stones in the background.*

of large slabs, which looks very much like an over-sized version of a hearth at Skara Brae. This would be entirely consistent with the idea of feasting in the circle, but the contents of the 'hearth' suggested that fire had been a minor element in its use. A post-hole to one side of the 'hearth' may have held a temporary 'totem-pole', as suggested in the artist's reconstruction of a ceremony held here (60). Based on the dog-bones found in the ditch, the reconstruction implies a special sanctity here for the dog, an ally both for the huntsman and, perhaps even at this early date, for the shepherd.

Between the central 'hearth' and the entrance through the ditch and bank were traces in the form of stone-holes of a pair of standing stones, together with the bedding-trench of what may have been a timber-built structure, and another setting of holes for upright stones. The second group of stone-holes showed that there had indeed existed some form of stone structure in the place where the 'altar' had been built in 1907.

Exactly what was its original appearance could not be established. After the excavation, the two upright stones were re-erected, and the horizontal slab lies beside them (**colour plate 6**).

Radiocarbon analysis of animal bones from the ditch and charcoal from the central stone setting indicates that the monument was in existence by 3000 BC. Sherds of incised Grooved Ware link the people who used this ceremonial structure with those living at the nearby Barnhouse settlement, as well as those living at Skara Brae. It is likely that people would have come from all over Orkney to attend appropriate gatherings here. We shall never know the whole story of how a circle-henge like this was used, and the truth was probably very complex. Human burial, animal sacrifice, feasting, dedicatory ceremonies, these can all be inferred from the evidence at various sites, but many activities would leave no physical trace. Music, dancing, teaching, prayers and the dispensation of communal justice are just some of the possibilities.

The early date for the Stones of Stenness came as a surprise, because it is earlier than many henges in mainland Britain. But this is perhaps confirmation that Orkney was not slow to adopt new ideas and may even have had a hand in the development of innovations usually attributed to an origin in southern England.

61 The Ring of Brodgar.

The Ring of Brodgar

The Brodgar circle was conceived on a grand scale. Although none of the stones stands as high as those at Stenness, their great number and and the vast circumference of the circle make this an awesome monument (**61**). There were originally 60 stones, of which the tallest surviving stone is 4.2m (14ft) high, and they form a ring 103.7m (340ft) in diameter. The layout of the Stones of Stenness is closer to an ellipse than to a true circle, but the Ring of Brodgar is a perfect circle, easier to appreciate from the air than on the ground (**colour plate 5**). It lies on a gentle slope, closer to the shore of the Loch of Harray than to the Loch of Stenness, and its encircling henge-ditch is sculpted out of the bedrock. Although partly filled with silt, the ditch is still a very marked feature at ground-level today; when first dug, its appearance must have been dramatic, for it was some 10m (33ft) across at the top and up to 3.4m (11ft) deep. There are two entrance-causeways across the ditch, one to the north-west and the other on the opposite south-eastern side.

Three trenches were excavated under the direction of Professor Colin Renfrew in 1973, two across the ditch and one placed outside the ditch to test whether there was any trace of a bank. The lower part of the rock-cut ditch had vertical sides, and the stones for the circle may

well have been quarried from it. There was plenty of space within the circle for the ditch-cutting and the setting up of the stones to have been carried out as one operation. There was no conclusive evidence for the former existence of an outer bank, but such a great volume of material would have been dug out of the ditch that a substantial bank seems inevitable.

It was estimated that some 4700 cubic metres (165,978 cu ft) of rock had been prised out of the ditch at Brodgar, compared with about 620 cubic metres (21,894 cu ft) from the ditch at Stenness. In terms of the human effort involved in these operations, the Brodgar ditch would have needed some 80,000 man-hours to complete the work, and the Stenness ditch some 12,500 man-hours. If the stones for the circle were derived from the ditch at Brodgar, they would have to be levered out and manoeuvred into position. The origin of the Stones of Stenness is uncertain, but they may have been quarried at Vestra Field, north of the Bay of Skaill, and transported on rollers over a distance of some 7½ miles to Stenness. There are certainly very large slabs lying on the surface at Vestra Field. But it is equally possible that they were quarried much closer to Stenness, from the lochside or by stripping the turf off any outcrop.

The limited excavations at the Ring of Brodgar yielded no evidence to date the construction of the monument, but it is likely to have been built during the early or middle centuries of the third millennium.

Only 17% of earthwork henges contain stone circles as at Stenness and Brodgar, but without excavation it is impossible to be sure that stones have not been removed. Circle-henges were certainly built throughout Britain, from Brodgar to Bodmin Moor in Cornwall. Too little is known about internal arrangements in circles to establish whether central stone settings are typical, and even at Stenness there may have been other structures in the large areas of the circle that were not excavated.

Building a stone circle

The first task in building a stone circle was probably to mark out the ring and to prepare the ground by stripping off the turf and soil. This was certainly done in the case of chambered tombs and houses, and the central stone setting at Stenness was sunk into the boulder clay in such a way that the tops of the slabs were flush with the natural surface. A perfect circle such as the Ring of Brodgar was a simple matter to achieve. A peg would be driven into the ground and a cord, perhaps made of animal skin, tied to it; by holding the other end of the cord taut and walking round in a circle, other pegs could be driven in to the ground to mark the circumference of the circle. Not all rings were perfect circles, however, and the mathematician, Professor Alexander Thom, has argued that more complicated figures such as ellipses were based on a knowledge of quite complex geometry. If he is right, Neolithic society in Britain understood the 5:12:13 triangle 2500 years before its theory was defined by Pythagoras. As a result of many years of measuring stone circles and alignments, Alexander Thom also argued that the builders of these monuments used a standard unit of measurement, which he named the 'megalithic yard'. This is the equivalent of 0.829m (2.72ft). The diameter of the Ring of Brodgar is exactly 125 megalithic yards.

After marking out the site, large holes would

be dug for the standing stones, large enough to take both the base of the stone and sufficient stone packing to wedge it firmly in place. The reconstruction drawing shows how the stones were probably set in place (**62**). Using a timber raft, the stone would gradually be levered up at one end until the other end was tipped into the hole. Ropes and a wooden framework known to us as shear-legs would allow control over the final stage of raising the stone into a vertical position and holding it there while large boulders were packed round its base.

52 Artist's reconstruction of the building of a stone circle, using a wooden framework to help raise each stone.

A more controversial aspect of Alexander Thom's work concerns the astronomical alignments that he attributed to megalithic monuments. Archaeologists are happy to accept that the major movements of the sun and moon were important to the prehistoric farming calendar and were recorded in stone. But problems arise with more complicated astronomical predictions. In some cases the interpretation calls for more detailed recording knowledge than is compatible with a non-literate society, while in others the astronomical chronology cannot be reconciled with the archaeological evidence. The Ring of Brodgar illustrates the latter problem. Alexander Thom argued that the circle and the mounds around it 'form the most complete Megalithic observatory remaining in Britain'. He argued that the Ring had been built on a slope rather than on level ground in order to allow observation of at least four lunar alignments between the centre of the circle and various hills on the horizon, via some of the mounds close to the circle. He calculated that this observatory was used to track the movements of the moon between about 1700 and 1400 BC. The problem for the archaeologist is that the circle-henge cannot possibly have been built at such a late date, although the burial mounds may belong to that period.

The passages of most chambered tombs were built facing the south-east quadrant of the compass, but there seems not to have been any very precise preference within that quadrant. This suggests that the builders were not aiming for an alignment on a particular celestial event, but rather on a more general observation probably connected with midwinter sunrise. Individual tombs may also have been aligned on more local factors, such as landmarks or visibility from settlements. There is no reason to expect that the stone circles should reflect any more sophisticated astronomical interest than this.

Social organization

The larger chambered tombs and the circle-henges represent an enormous investment of time and labour in building public works. Colin Renfrew based his estimates of labour requirements on data for quarrying by traditional methods in Orkney in relatively recent times, and he allowed for the extra time needed for work undertaken with primitive equipment. He estimated that digging the ditch at Brodgar would take 100 men some 100 days, after which there would be the incalculable task of raising the stones. Nothing is known of the interior of the circle; a geophysical survey produced little information and there has been no excavation. The construction of Maes Howe is likely to have been an even greater task, in view of the fact that the stone would have to be transported to the site.

Compared with earlier and smaller chambered tombs, the three monuments of Brodgar, Stenness and Maes Howe involved in their construction and presumably also in their use larger numbers of people and greater organization. Colin Renfrew has argued that society in Orkney evolved from one based on small individual and independent communities to one based on an overall centralized organization. Only in this latter type of chiefdom society could the whole population have been involved in the investment of labour represented by the major public monuments. John Hedges developed the argument further by suggesting that, as the labour-investment in monuments increased, the geographical territories of the communities involved also grew larger as tribal units merged together. This attractive hypothesis relies, unfortunately, on making assumptions about the dating of chambered tombs.

Standing stones in the Brodgar-Stenness area

The Watch Stone is aptly named, for it stands guard over the Stenness end of the causeway

81

linking the two promontories. At 5.6m (19ft) high, it matches the tallest of the stones in the nearby circle. It was once one of a pair, but its mate no longer survives; the stump of a standing stone was found many years ago to the south-south-west of the Watch Stone. Both should probably be seen as outliers of the Stenness circle, and they may have marked a ceremonial way between Stenness and the Ring of Brodgar. The famous but sadly long-since vanished Stone of Odin stood to the north of the Stones of Stenness. It was destroyed in 1814 (p.11) but the hole in which it had been set was discovered a few years ago.

On the Ness of Brodgar, there are several standing stones which may be connected with a ceremonial way between the two circles. There is

a danger in assuming that all these monuments belong to the same date, and standing stones are notoriously difficult to date. Excavation round the base of the stone has a very small chance of recovering organic material for scientific dating. Nevertheless, it seems reasonable to envisage that people continued to add to the monuments in this important area over the centuries. If the path between the two circles was not marked by standing stones from the beginning, it certainly was at a later date, perhaps towards the end of the third millennium.

Just beyond the causeway on the Ness of Brodgar is a pair of stones set 8.3m (27ft) apart along the side of the ridge. Closer to the Ring of Brodgar is a curious monument known as the Comet Stone (63). In times past, Brodgar was popularly thought to be the temple of the sun and Stenness, apparently a crescent of stones, to be the temple of the moon. The Comet Stone was perhaps thought to represent a celestial comet. It

63 Part of the Ring of Brodgar with the Comet Stone in the middle distance.

A pair of standing stones at Deepdale may have been part of the Brodgar-Stenness complex. One of the pair survives today, standing on the slope above the south-east side of the Loch of Stenness and visible across the water from Brodgar. Like the Maes Howe-Barnhouse Stone alignment, the Brodgar-Deepdale alignment may have been associated with the setting sun. Another standing stone is set on Staney Hill on the east side of the Loch of Harray, and there may have been others in the area that have not survived.

Orcadian society

There are chiefs and chiefs. If Orcadian society in the later Neolithic period was moving towards centralized organization, it is tempting to see in this the emergence of individual power. It would seem particularly appropriate to interpret Maes Howe as a grand gesture by a ruling élite, the Orcadian equivalent of an Egyptian Pharoah's pyramid. But is this concept of a all-powerful lord really suited to the evidence in Orkney? Maes Howe was certainly special, but it was still designed with side-cells for multiple burials. If only those burials had survived! If they were all adult males or all adult females, we should have a fine basis for argument. The outsized house at Barnhouse could have been the home of a chief, but it could equally well have been a ceremonial meeting-house for certain people or for the whole village. For all the special character of two of the buildings at Skara Brae, there is no reason to suppose that the village was not entirely egalitarian. Power and authority can be expressed through a group of people, a council of elders perhaps, and still command allegiance over a wide area and many communities. There may be a chief, but he or she works according to the common decisions of the group.

Dealing with a non-literate society at this remove of time, we cannot expect to identify the niceties of the social system. Archaeology can recognize the physical attributes of a particular society through buildings and artefacts, and here

64 *The Barnhouse Stone.*

stands on a low circular platform, and stumps survive of two other stones set at right angles to the Comet.

Farther afield from the centre of the ceremonial complex are several standing stones. There seems to have been a connection between the standing stone known as the Barnhouse Stone (**64**) and the tomb of Maes Howe. When the setting sun at midwinter shines down the passage into the chamber, its rays come in directly over the Barnhouse Stone, the top of which is 3.2m (10ft) high. This suggests either that the standing stone was part of the original plan when the tomb was built, or that the stone was set up subsequently to emphasize the orientation of the tomb. The fact that recent excavations uncovered the hole for a standing stone immediately outside the tomb (p.57) lends support to the idea that the Barnhouse Stone was closely involved in ceremonies taking place at Maes Howe.

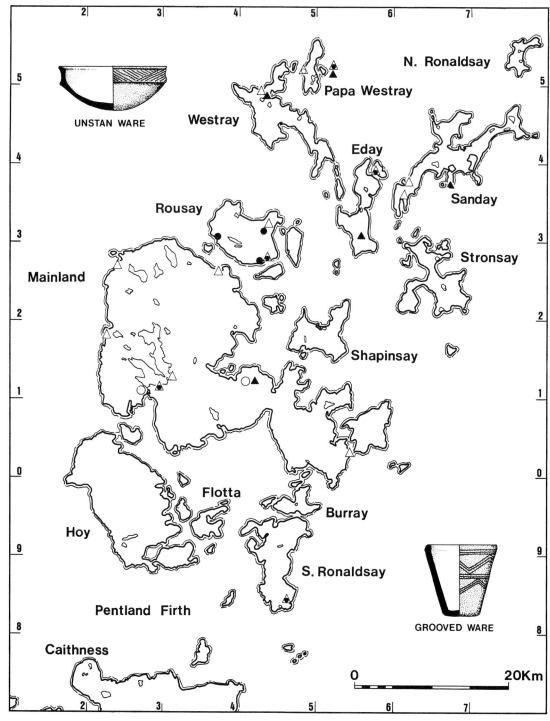

UNSTAN WARE

GROOVED WARE

0   20Km

○ Unstan Ware Settlements

● Stalled And Related Tombs

△ Unstan Ware Settlements With Grooved Ware

▲ Stalled Tomb with Grooved Ware Or Related
   Artifacts

△ Grooved Ware Settlements

▲ Maes Howe Type Tombs

Neolithic Orkney presents an intriguing problem. The previous three chapters have described the settlements and tombs of two apparently distinct cultural groups: those using Unstan Ware and those using Grooved Ware (65). The first group lived in individual family farmsteads (though this is based on just one site), used Unstan Ware and some characteristic artefacts and buried their dead in stalled cairns. The second group lived in small villages, used Grooved Ware and some characteristic artefacts, buried their dead in Maes Howe-type tombs and built henges. As Grooved Ware and henges were common throughout mainland Britain, it would be a simple solution to regard this group as intrusive into Orkney, but the situation is more complicated. Maes Howe-type tombs appear to have been a local invention, for they were unique to Orkney and the few artefacts found in them link them firmly to Grooved Ware settlements and henges.

Moreover, there seems to have been a degree of overlap between the two communities both in time and in artefacts. Although the radiocarbon dates suggest that the farm at Knap of Howar was founded some four centuries before the earliest Grooved Ware village or tomb, thereafter the two cultural groups existed side by side. Some Grooved Ware features occur in assemblages of Unstan Ware pottery, and some specialized tools are shared by both groups. But Grooved Ware pottery and artefacts only occur outside stalled cairns or associated with their final closure, and Unstan Ware is never associated with Maes Howe-type tombs.

The results of excavations at Pool in Sanday may well help to clarify the relationship between these two cultural groups. This was a domestic settlement on the west coast of the island. The remains of some 14 Neolithic buildings were found during work in the 1980s, together with a complex series of midden deposits. A very large

quantity of pottery was recovered, which consisted of sherds from about 1900 vessels, and the sequence of pot-shapes and decoration will provide a useful yardstick for other sites. The earliest levels yielded round-based vessels, mostly plain but including some decorated Unstan bowls. These were replaced in the second phase by flat-based vessels with incised decoration, made from clay with shell-temper. In the third and latest phase, there was a complete change in the shape, decoration and fabric of the vessels. This new pottery was bucket-shaped and more commonly decorated with applied motifs than with incised designs, and the clay fabric was tempered with rock grit. Both the incised and applied decoration of the second and third phases is Grooved Ware, but the fabric in phase 2 is closer to that of phase 1. In other words, this seems to demonstrate a sequence from Unstan Ware to incised Grooved Ware and thence, with significant changes, to Grooved Ware with applied decoration. The incised Grooved Ware has also been found at the Barnhouse settlement, the adjacent Stones of Stenness and the early Maes Howe-type tomb at Quanterness. Both incised and applied decoration occur at Skara Brae and Rinyo, but only applied decoration at the late settlement at Links of Noltland.

There is thus a chronological sequence from Unstan Ware to Grooved Ware, which confirms not only the link between them but also the local development of the pan-British Grooved Ware fashion.

It seems clear that the Grooved Ware community gained ascendancy over the older Unstan Ware users, but essentially they may both have embodied another expression of the concept of duality. For whatever reason, some people adhered to one tradition and some to the other. Perhaps, since the right-hand appears to have been an important factor of access into Grooved Ware houses, Unstan Ware represented the left-hand, the female. Could there have been a social change from a matriarchal to a patriarchal system? Perhaps this is going beyond the proper bounds of archaeological evidence.

65 Map showing discoveries of Unstan Ware and Grooved Ware in settlements and tombs in Orkney.

CHAPTER SIX

A prehistoric recession?

Orcadians seem to have gone into a period of economic recession towards the end of the third millennium BC. There were new social and technological developments in mainland Scotland which appear not to have reached Orkney in full force, but neither did they reach Caithness, Sutherland or the far west, and the question is, why not? To answer that question, we need to look at what was happening in the rest of Britain.

From about 2700 BC, there was a major technological advance in the form of metalworking, a new skill introduced from Europe, where in the Balkans it had already been practised for some 2000 years. Initially, gold was worked into personal ornaments and copper was used for axes and daggers, but copper is relatively soft and was soon alloyed with tin to make a stronger metal, bronze. At the same time, a new type of pottery began to appear in distinctive graves, and again the impetus came from Europe. Beakers are highly decorated fine pottery, thought to have been drinking vessels (and there is some evidence to suggest that they were used for alcoholic drinks made from honey and herbs). An idealized impression of a beaker grave can be seen in the artist's reconstruction (66). The body is placed on its side with knees drawn up, strewn with flowers, and alongside it lie a beaker, a bow and quiver full of arrows and a bronze dagger in its sheath of animal skin. The idea of an individual grave with personal grave-goods contrasts strongly with the old traditions of communal burial in chambered tombs.

In Scotland, beaker burials and early bronze artefacts are common discoveries in the south and east but rare in the west and north. Should we expect a uniform distribution? The earliest types of beaker in Scotland match up with styles which indicate contact directly across the North Sea from the Low Countries. The nature of this contact was not simply exchange of goods, for there is evidence of limited immigration of people, and some immigration may also have been involved in the introduction of metalworking skills. There is some argument among archaeologists about the scale of the immigration. Study of the skeletal remains in early beaker graves has indicated that there was a difference in physique between them and the older population, in that they were a little taller with broader heads, but there is a tendency now to argue that this may have been the result of genetic changes in the existing population. In eastern Scotland, there is unfortunately too little bone material from the older population to compare with the skeletons found in beaker graves. Nevertheless, the overall impression from bones, artefacts and grave rites supports the idea that some immigration of people took place in the later centuries of the third millennium.

Their number was probably never great and their influence was naturally strongest in the area in which they settled. This may explain why beaker pottery is rarely found north of the Dornoch Firth, but it can hardly explain why the

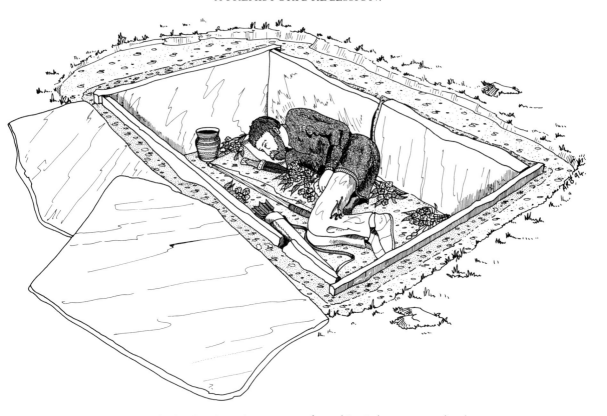

66 *Artist's reconstruction of a beaker burial in a cist.*

population farther north was not more anxious to acquire bronze artefacts. A beaker one could do without, but a bronze axe would be a practical as well as a prestigious asset. Given the poor quality of local flint, the advantages of bronze ought to have been all the more desirable, unless there were economic or social reasons that made the acquisition of metal goods difficult or unacceptable. In southern England, the early beaker burials are found well away from the ceremonial centres of the older population, as if in social terms the two were incompatible. A similar situation in Orkney would account for the apparent isolation of the islands until well into the Bronze Age. In addition, a long period of climatic deterioration began around 2000 BC, and this would have made sea-travel more difficult and would have contributed to the isolation of the islands.

Although no classic beaker burial has been found in Orkney, some beaker pottery was in use both here and farther north in Shetland, and the Northern Isles were thus participating to some extent in the new developments, if rather later than in mainland Scotland. Mostly it is broken sherds of beakers that turn up, rather than complete vessels, and they are found in or around chambered tombs as part of the activities involved either in the closure of the tombs or outside the tombs. Until recent excavations, beaker sherds had been found only inside the chambers at Knowe of Yarso and Calf of Eday Long. This is probably because most excavators concentrated on the tomb interior, whereas modern excavation also involves the immediate environment of the tomb. Beaker sherds were discovered outside the entrance into the tomb at Howe and alongside the cairn at Holm of Papa Westray North. Grooved Ware has also been found in secondary contexts outside tombs, and part of a beaker was uncovered in the doorway into one of the houses belonging to the makers of Grooved Ware at Rinyo in Rousay. But mostly the two types of pottery and the social traditions that they represent occur separately.

The only complete beaker was discovered in a cist at Newhouse in Birsay, but unfortunately soil conditions were such that the bones did not survive. This is a small and late type of beaker, decorated with incised lines of zig-zag which show a lasting local taste for this motif. The idea of burial in a cist became the norm in Orkney as elsewhere, for this was a development that was not confined to those with a taste for beakers and their alcoholic beverages.

Early metalworking

Bronze is an alloy of copper and tin, and it is an extraordinary fact that tin could be obtained in Britain only in Cornwall, with the result that bronze-workers were dependent from the start upon long-distance trade or exchange contacts. Copper was less of a problem, although little is known about how or where it was obtained. Copper ore occurs in several places in Orkney (see **6**), but there are records of only two sources having been exploited in the recent past, in Burray and in Rousay, and there is no evidence to prove that any were worked in prehistoric times. Nevertheless, distinctive types of bronze artefact have been found in Orkney which demonstrate that the products of the new technology were appreciated soon after its introduction into Scotland before 2000 BC. It is more difficult to find evidence of the metalworking process; part of a stone mould for an axe found a century ago somewhere in Orkney suggests the presence of a craftsman, but it is a solitary find and cannot imply more than the fleeting presence of a craftsman.

Unfortunately, most of the discoveries of bronze artefacts were accidental and nothing is known about their context, neither whether they were part of a settlement or a burial, nor whether they were genuine losses or deliberate deposits. One of the finest artefacts is a remarkably complete dagger, which was found during peat cutting in Flanders Moss, Wasbister, Rousay, in 1905. The damp conditions in the peat preserved the horn hilt, which was carved as a single piece and then split at the base to take the top of the bronze blade; three bronze rivets fasten the hilt and blade together, and the edges of the blade show signs of having been sharpened on a whetstone many times. The top of the hilt was carved into a tang which would have been inserted into a pommel, but this did not survive or was perhaps missing. This was surely a prestigious piece of personal equipment. Most such daggers found in Scotland come from graves belonging in date to the early part of the bronze age, and some have traces of the leather sheaths in which they were kept. The Orkney dagger sounds like a genuine loss, for it is dated earlier than the growth of peat and was presumably lying in the turf when the peat began to form.

Axes are by far the most common product of bronze-working, and it is a measure of how few early bronze artefacts have been found in Orkney that only three are axes (and there is some doubt as to whether two of them really came from the islands). One is a type known as a flanged axe, because the butt has projecting flanges to ensure a safer anchorage in the haft; the reconstruction shows such an axe lashed within the split end of a wooden haft (**67**). This particular type of flanged axe has been found most commonly around the Firth of Forth in south-east Scotland, and the Orkney example indicates some sort of contact between the two areas. Compared with the numbers of bronze artefacts found in mainland Scotland, the few from Orkney suggest a degree of isolation, or at least conservatism, throughout much of the second millennium. This impression is not confined to bronzework, for the islands also lack much evidence of the pottery fashionable farther south, such as beakers and distinctive types of cinerary urn. There are occasional and notable exceptions; the Rousay dagger is one, and another is a tiny decorated bowl known as an accessory cup. This was found in South Ronaldsay, probably associated with a burial, and it is likely to have been imported from farther south.

Knowes of Trotty

Most remarkable of all is a rich burial in central mainland Orkney which would not have been out of place among the princely graves of southern England at this period. At the foot of the steep western slope of the Ward of Redland, east of the Loch of Harray, is a group of burial mounds arranged in two rows, known as the Knowes of Trotty. The largest mound lies at the north end of one of the rows; it is about 18m (60ft) across and 3m (10ft) high on a low platform. George Petrie dug into the mound in 1858 and discovered a stone cist containing burnt human bones and, placed on a flat slab in one corner, four gold discs (**colour plate 7**, and **back cover**) and 21 pieces of amber. The discs were made from thin sheets of gold, with

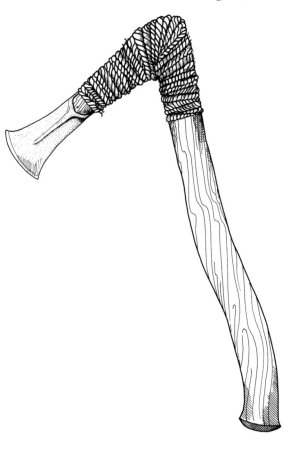

67 Artist's reconstruction of a flanged bronze axe in its handle.

concentric circles of decoration consisting of bands of zig-zag and oblique or right-angle lines between raised ribs. Such discs have been found elsewhere covering conical buttons, and this is likely to have been the purpose here; if the buttons had been made of wood, they would not have survived. Unfortunately there are no details recorded of the exact shape in which the discs were found. Their decoration is very similar to that on the little incense cup from South Ronaldsay. One example of a conical button has been found in Orkney; made of jet, it was part of the hoard of objects found outside the chambered tomb at Isbister in South Ronaldsay (p.54).

The technical aspects of the decoration on the gold discs links them with goldwork produced in Wessex in southern England, but analysis of the gold itself has emphasized a Scottish source. There is an unusual amount of tin in the gold, not enough to argue deliberate inclusion by the goldsmith but enough to suggest that the gold ore came from an unlocated Scottish source in which there was already a trace of tin. The same ore seems to have been used for a decorative band on the hilt of a bronze dagger from Collessie in Fife.

The amber pieces included two circular beads, two hook-shaped pendants and seventeen triangular or fragmentary rectangular plates. The latter are perforated and were originally part of a type of necklace known as a spacer-plate necklace, which was made in the early part of the Bronze Age in amber in southern Britain and in jet in the north. Here the spacer-plates appear to have been cut up and re-used simply as beads, perhaps the remnant of a valued heirloom. Amber is the resin of trees that grew in eastern Sweden and southern Finland many thousands of years ago when what is now the Baltic Sea was dry land. Deposits of this resin were subsequently dispersed and, although some amber reached the east coast of Britain, most of that used in Britain in prehistoric times will have been imported from across the North Sea. Thus the amber from the Knowes of Trotty had a long and much-travelled history, imported from

Scandinavia into southern Britain where it was made into a spacer-plate necklace and eventually taken north to Orkney. The gold discs are likely also to have been heirloom pieces, and neither they nor the amber can be used to date the grave closely, though both suggest that the person buried had been of considerable social standing.

The other ten burial mounds at Knowes of Trotty show signs of having been opened at some stage but no records survive of what was found. The rich burial that Petrie found is likely to have been the earliest, for such linear barrow-cemeteries sometimes have a founder grave at one end which is also the largest mound.

Some 250 barrows and cairns have been recorded in Orkney, both isolated and in groups, along with another 100 short cists, most of which probably belonged to this period. The difference between a barrow and a cairn is that the former was built essentially of earth and the latter of stones. Short cists are rectangular stone-lined boxes in which a human body had to be folded into a crouched position, whereas the later long cists of the first millennium AD could hold an outstretched body and were the equivalent of coffins. Very few of these burial places have been excavated in modern times, although many have been explored in the past with varying degrees of recording. The burial was not always of a single individual, for some cists held the remains of more than one person, and some cists that were not buried beneath a mound may have been used on more than one occasion.

What Orkney lacks in the way of fashionable artefacts is compensated by a unique variety of short cists. In addition to the basic stone box, there are two-storey cists, in one case the upper compartment divided into two by a medial slab, cists built of a combination of upright slabs and horizontal walling, and cists of even more elaborate design. One at Quandale in Rousay had a small inner cist built against one side, and another at Orphir had a small extension off one side in which there were several skulls, almost a miniature version of a chambered tomb with a side cell.

Sand Fiold

An important focus of burials in the second millennium seems to have been the sand-dunes behind Skaill Bay in western mainland, an area known as Sand Fiold. The mounds here were sufficiently prominent to have attracted the attention of Sir Joseph Banks when he visited Orkney in 1772 on his way back from Iceland; in the words of Reverend George Low of Stromness, 'One day in Particular we went a Grave Digging in the Links of Skail on the mainland where there are great numbers of tumuli'. They opened at least two mounds, one of which contained two tiers of cist burials, and one yielded a necklace of jet beads.

The most extraordinary burial, however, was found more than 200 years later when a lorry sank into a hole in a sand quarry, revealing a subterranean rock-cut chamber fully 2m (6½ft) deep and 3.3m (11ft) square. Within the chamber had been built a very large free-standing cist, set to one side to leave space for people to enter the chamber from above, through the capstones, and open the side of the cist. The 'door' to the cist was most ingenious, consisting of a single slab which could be 'locked' into position by a small stone wedged into the bottom right-hand corner (**68**).

There were three separate burial deposits. The earliest seems to have been the cremated remains of an adult aged 25–40 years, which had been placed inside a woven grass basket inside a large pottery urn; this was standing upright in one corner at the back of the cist. In the other corner at the back were the unburnt bones of an adult, probably a female, and an eight-month-old foetus, suggesting that the pair had died in childbirth. In the centre of the cist was a pile of cremated bones, apparently covered by the remains of some sort of mat; the bones proved to belong to an adult male of 25–30 years. A series of radiocarbon dates from the various organic deposits indicates that the cist was in use around 2000 BC.

Nothing like this has been found before. The

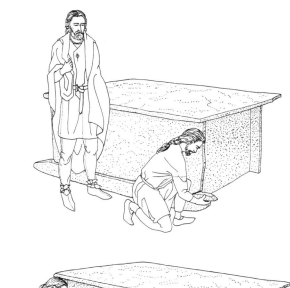

68 Artist's reconstruction of how the side of the cist at Sand Fiold could be opened.

fact that the cist could be used more than once harks back to the tradition of chambered tombs, some of which were still being used as late as the end of the third millennium and many of which would still have been prominent and recognizable in the landscape. One is left wondering what else may be hidden beneath the sand-dunes of Sand Fiold.

Modern excavations such as this demonstrate how much more information can be retrieved with refined methods of excavation and post-excavation analysis, particularly where elusive organic materials are involved.

The Sand Fiold cist was free-standing within its chamber. An earthen mound excavated in 1990 at Mousland, north-west of Stromness, revealed a small central burial cist built at ground-level, its upright slabs supported by clay

before the covering mound was built. Cists constructed at ground-level rather than sunk into a pit are a common occurrence in Orkney. The stone kerb of the mound had also been built as a free-standing structure of four courses of drystone walling before the mound had been added. The cist held the cremated remains of an adult female, and radiocarbon analysis indicated a date for the burial around 1800 BC. There was also evidence of the contemporary environment, showing that the mound had been built amongst open grassland and heathland, away from the contemporary agricultural land. An earlier land surface indicated, however, that the land had once been cultivated, perhaps even over-cultivated leading to loss of fertility.

The ceremonial heartland of Brodgar–Stenness–Maes Howe became a focus for burials in the second millennium, and there were once even more mounds than survive today, for many have been flattened by ploughing. One large and six or more small barrows clustered close to Maes Howe, and some very large barrows can still be seen near the Ring of Brodgar, along with a number of smaller barrows. Close to the shore of the loch to the north-west of the Ring is a distinctive type of barrow rare in Scotland but common in southern England. Its presence here underlines the link between the two areas already seen in the finds from the Knowes of Trotty. Known as a disc barrow, the burial mound is surrounded by a circular bank, the earth for which was scraped up from the space between the bank and the mound. The whole monument is an impressive 30m (98ft) in diameter. Another disc barrow lies on the east side of the Loch of Harray, a little to the north of Maes Howe.

Groups of small burial mounds are common in Orkney, as are discoveries of cists whose mounds have been ploughed away, and excavation of such a cemetery of barrows at Quoyscottie near Dounby demonstrated that there can also be less formal burials of cremations in simple small pits associated with such barrow cemeteries. An experiment was carried out at

Quoyscottie to prove whether a body could be cremated adequately on an open-air pyre; a goat weighing four stones was burned on an open pyre, and it took five hours for the body to be reduced to ash and fragments of burnt bone. An adult human body weighing twice as much or more would take longer, but it could be done. As ever in the Northern Isles the problem lies in fuel. During the First World War, the standard allowance for the cremation of Indian soldiers was one ton of wood, which would have been an unthinkable waste of a valuable resource in Orkney and Shetland.

Many archaeological sites in Orkney, both domestic and funerary, have produced a burnt material known as 'cramp', a crumbly glassy substance. Examples have been analysed on several occasions without satisfactory conclusions, but it seems possible that this substance results from burning dried seaweed, along with the sand adhering to it, on a turf surface. Seaweed is the one plentiful fuel in Orkney and may well have been used in this way.

In many cases cremation burials were placed inside urns carved out of steatite, a soft stone also known as soapstone. The nearest source of this stone is Shetland, and its presence in Orkney implies import through barter or exchange of gifts; the vessels were presumably carved in Shetland. Steatite urns were certainly used for contemporary burials in Shetland.

Orcadians may not have been frequent customers of the bronze trade but they were certainly keen to be seen as keeping up with new fashions in weapons, even if it meant copying them in another material. A farmer digging peat in the summer of 1957 came across a wooden sword, a careful replica of the earliest type of bronze sword to be made in Britain (**69**). Although a wooden sword may not seem a very effective weapon, this one is carved from yew, which is a heavy and very dense wood and may have made a serviceable, if club-like, weapon. The blade is 0.7m (2ft 4in) long and undamaged but the hilt is worn, indicating considerable use which continued even after the pommel had broken off. It may have been used in some ceremonial way and it may well have been thrown deliberately into a boggy pool as an offering. It was found in deep peat near the farm of Grotsetter in Tankerness.

The bronze versions of this type of sword were made in the early centuries of the first millennium BC and, although none has been found in Orkney, two have been discovered in Caithness. More significant perhaps is the fact that the Grotsetter sword was made of yew, for this wood is unlikely to have been growing in Orkney; its northern limit today is in Perthshire. The sword was presumably imported ready-carved.

Curiously, the area of Orkney in which the sword was found, the parish of St Andrews and Deerness south-east of Kirkwall, has also

69 *A wooden version of a bronze sword.*

produced most of the contemporary bronze artefacts, again mostly found in peat-cutting. They include socketed knives, a razor and a socketed axe. It is difficult to explain why the area should apparently be important at this period, and it may be that the discoveries of artefacts are related more to intensive exploitation of the peat than to any real concentration of buying-power in the late Bronze Age. If this is correct, there ought to be many more artefacts to be discovered elsewhere and to alter the impression of a relatively isolated community. The two socketed knives belong to a type more common in southern England than in the north, suggesting that the link between Orkney and the south may still have been in operation.

The disaster theory

There was a huge eruption of the volcano Hekla in Iceland in 1159 BC. The dust or tephra that was ejected up into the atmosphere spread over a very wide area and had a devastating effect on the climate; a fine layer of tephra has been identified on archaeological sites in western and northern Scotland, and in Ireland the growth-rings in oak wood preserved in bogs show a dramatic band of very narrow rings beginning in 1159, the result of exceptionally poor growing seasons. Pollen analysis of samples from Caithness has demonstrated that pine made up almost 20% of the total of pollen before the Hekla eruption and that it plummetted to less than 2% afterwards. Scholars have argued that this spectacular deterioration in the climate had an appalling effect upon living conditions in the British Isles, particularly upon those people farming in upland areas that were already marginal in terms of a viable economy. Even before the tree-ring and tephra evidence had been recognized, Colin Burgess had suggested on archaeological evidence that there had been a dramatic drop in the population of Britain in the twelfth century BC, somewhere in the region of three million halving to one and a half million, and that the population did not recover until

around the middle of the first millennium BC. To take just one aspect of the archaeological evidence, the bronze industry, there was a marked decline in the production of axes in the twelfth and eleventh centuries and, at the same time, a wider range of weapons; Colin Burgess relates this phenomenon to the fierce competition for land and resources that resulted from the climatic disaster.

How did the disaster affect Orkney? It accelerated the growth of blanket peat, which in the long term was an advantage in providing vital fuel; the immediate effect is harder to gauge, but there is little evidence of widespread field walls buried beneath peat which elsewhere points to abandonment of upland areas. This may however be an illusion created by the lack of archaeological (rather than palaeobotanical) work on Orcadian bogs, for early field walls have been identified beneath peat in Eday and no doubt exist elsewhere. Large-scale land boundaries known as trebs survive, probably from this period; they consist of substantial earthen banks which divide up the islands into large blocks of land. Two trebs traverse the island of North Ronaldsay, dividing it into three portions, and sections of one, known as the Muckle Gairsty, are particularly well-preserved and fully 11m (36ft) wide at the base. This seems unnecessarily wasteful of land and more formidable than a land boundary need be, and there may be more to trebs than is possible now to appreciate.

Too few settlements of the period are known to allow any conclusions to be drawn about population trends, and there are too few bronze artefacts to show any real change in the market other than that new forms of weapons appear around 1000 BC. It may not be a coincidence, however, that a new type of domestic site became common in Orkney in this period – the burnt mound.

Burnt mounds

The essence of a burnt mound is that it is composed of burnt stones and dark soil containing charcoal and ash, although at first glance it looks much like any other grass and heather-covered mound. They are mostly to be found close to a source of water and many are crescentic in shape and irregular in outline. Classic examples can be seen south of Dounby (Fan Knowe) and at Backiskaill in Papa Westray, and many others are marked on the Ordnance Survey Landranger maps. The burnt stones are in fact the waste product from a cooking technique which involved heating stones in a hearth and dropping them into a tank of water; once the water boiled, joints of meat wrapped in straw or a skin could be cooked in it. The hard sandstone of Orkney was particularly suitable, because it tended to crack rather than shatter when heated and quenched. This is an age-old method of cooking which survived in the Hebrides at least into the eighteenth century, for it answered the problem of how to boil food if pottery was not strong enough and metal containers were too expensive. The tank could be a solid wooden trough or, more commonly in Orkney, a pit lined with stone slabs and made water-tight by sealing the corners with clay.

Despite excavations and cooking experiments in Ireland, little interest was shown in burnt mounds in Scotland until the 1970s when one was excavated at Liddle in South Ronaldsay. The farmer, Ronald Simison, who excavated the chambered cairn of Isbister, had been using the mound as a quarry for road-metalling until he came across some sort of stone structure. He drew it to the attention of Colin Renfrew, who was then excavating at Quanterness, and the structure was examined by John Hedges, a member of his team. Set to one side of the mound, it proved to be oval in shape with an irregular wall and an entrance opening towards the edge of the mound. Inside, the working area was roughly paved and furnished with a hearth recessed into the wall and a large central tank sunk into the floor and lined with stones. John Hedges interpreted the whole structure as a house, but it is as likely that the wall was little more than a revetment against the burnt stones

70 *Artist's reconstruction of a cooking place; stones are being heated on the hearth ready to drop into the water-tank and the discarded stones are building up to form a burnt mound. Joints of meat lie wrapped in readiness for boiling.*

which steadily accumulated round the cooking area. Had it been roofed, the steam and heat would have been unbearable – some people have even suggested that it was a sauna! The drawing shows how such a structure might have developed and how such cooking places were used (**70**). Artefacts such as hammerstones, pot-lids and pottery from Liddle emphasize the domestic aspect of the site, and the presence of stone ard-shares indicates agricultural activity in the vicinity. The structure and its burnt mound have been preserved for visitors to see.

There are some 230 burnt mounds in Orkney distributed throughout mainland and most of the islands, and almost as many in Shetland, mostly in southern and western mainland, in both cases situated in areas of reasonably good agricultural land. The original figures were probably considerably higher, because these sites were thought to be of little interest and many have been destroyed. In size the mounds vary from a few metres across to 30m (98ft) or more, according to the length of time over which they were used. Experiments have shown that a single boiling produces around half a cubic metre of burnt stones, which means that the smallest mounds may have been the result of perhaps four or five boilings, whereas the large mounds represent several hundred. Were these communal cooking places and where did the community live? Historical records of early Irish society make it clear that such cooking places were used communally after the hunt, and, although hunting on any scale is unlikely to have been part of the tradition behind the Orcadian burnt mounds, communal feasting may well have been customary, perhaps bringing together a widely scattered group of people.

Burnt mounds occur in other areas of the British Isles at various dates from the early

second millennium BC into the medieval period, but in the Northern Isles they appear to begin around 1200 and not to extend much beyond the middle of the first millennium BC. Peat was the predominant fuel used and, although there were local pockets of peat by 1200, larger deposits would have been available in the following millennium when there was wide-spread blanket peat.

Compared with the architectural achievements of the fourth and earlier third millennium and those that were to follow in the first millennium, Orkney's Bronze Age seems a dull time and has certainly not left many monuments at which to marvel. But there were highlights, such as the great cist at Sand Fiold, and the gleam of gold and amber from the Knowes of Trotty hints of moments of glory.

CHAPTER SEVEN

Patrons and warlords

Excavations often produce surprises. In 1973 when Colin Renfrew was excavating the entrance to the chambered cairn at Quanterness, there appeared to be a semi-circular forecourt in front of the entrance. The excavated area was extended the following summer, and the 'forecourt' was revealed as a roundhouse built some two thousand years after the tomb itself (71). The cairn must by then have appeared as a huge grassy mound – and a handy source of building material. The entrance area of the cairn was dismantled and a large circular house was constructed, nestling into the side of the cairn. Was it intentional or accidental that the house was built at the entrance to the old tomb?

The house was about 7m (23ft) in diameter with a wall which was initially some 0.8m (2ft 8in) thick and was later widened round its outer part by additional stonework; this had the effect of lengthening the entrance passage and making the house appear even more substantial. It is the size and solidity of such houses, as well as their shape, that earn them the archaeological term 'roundhouse', and they were an innovation of the first millennium BC. Quanterness is the earliest such roundhouse known at present in Orkney, with radiocarbon dates suggesting that the primary occupation of the house took place around 700 BC. It appears from evidence of rebuilding and radiocarbon analysis to have remained in use for some 500 years or more, though there may have been periods of abandonment.

Part of an even more substantial roundhouse dating to around 600 BC was salvaged from the quarry at Pierowall in Westray, built on top of an earlier Neolithic chambered tomb (p.66). Contemporary with Pierowall was a circular building at Bu, near Stromness, again a rescue excavation but also a site that has aroused some controversy. This time the wall was preserved to a height of 1.5m (5ft) and its core was 3m (10ft) thick, but an inner and an outer face had been added, increasing the width to more than 5m (16ft). The inner face was an early addition and probably part of the initial building programme, but the outer cladding overlay midden material and must have been added later (unless the midden was spread there deliberately as some ritual part of the original building process). Could this have been a regular roundhouse which was later transformed into an even more substantial edifice? The interior was about 9m (30ft) in diameter and was furnished from the start with some finesse (72). The dominant feature was a huge semi-circular hearth with a stone kerb and a built-in water tank at one side; outside the hearth were littered domestic tools and many burnt pebbles which had probably been heated in the hearth and used to boil water in the tank for cooking. All this occupied the central area of the room, while round the wall there were compartments partitioned one from another by low upright slabs. Some were paved while others had earthen floors; most finds came from the small unpaved compartments and the

71 (Above) *The round-house at Quanterness; the striped pole marks the entrance of earlier tomb.*

72 (Below) *Inside the round-house at Bu during excavation; half of semi-circular hearth is emptied.*

adjacent central area, but they give no clue as to how each compartment might have been used.

Like Quanterness, the Bu building appears to have continued in use, though in modified form, over a long period; there is no close dating evidence to show quite how long, but 500–600 years seem possible.

More helpful in understanding how building traditions in the first millennium BC progressed was the excavation at Howe near Stromness. On the same site as the chambered tomb already described (p.57), domestic settlement was founded probably in the eighth century BC, beginning with a group of small houses within an enclosure and leading on to a roundhouse and thence to a broch. Here there is clear evidence that the roundhouse lay within a walled and ditched enclosure. The width of the roundhouse wall was very close to the first stage of building at Bu, and the floor area was divided, again like Bu, into compartments by radial partitions.

None of these roundhouses is now visible, but they have been described here in some detail, because, as a group, they are an important stage in the local architectural development that led to the broch.

The decision to build these distinctive and substantial roundhouses must signal some sort of social change. Its inception coincides with a period in which, elsewhere in Scotland, the bronze industry expanded, producing large numbers of weapons, and fortifications were built. These developments have been linked with evidence for climatic deterioration and consequent changes in land-use to suggest that competition for good land led to a more aggressive society. As discussed in the last chapter, there is little information about Orkney's participation in the bronze industry or trade, but there are more bronze artefacts dating from the early centuries of the first millennium BC than from the preceding millennium. There are certainly promontory forts, but none has been excavated and nothing is known of their date. There is no reason why social development in Orkney should necessarily have followed the same

pattern as elsewhere, but some significance must attach to the fact that roundhouses appear here at the same time broadly as evidence for social change elsewhere. We are left with the roundhouses themselves as an expression of the households that built and inhabited them. The large scale of these houses and the monumental physical appearance of those with thick walls suggest a desire to be seen as set apart from the bulk of the population, whether to convey power or prestige or some other special status.

This impression is strengthened by the architectural development that followed, for around the second or third century BC, the roundhouse was replaced by a taller and even more impressive version – the broch.

Brochs

Archaeologists are at their happiest when dealing with lots of the same thing. If a fashion in pottery can be recognized, or if a particular architectural design was repeatedly used, the archaeologist has a sense of past community spirit, whereas an oddity leaves a trail of unanswerable questions. The broch is an example of an ancient monument which is both highly distinctive and profuse and which ought to allow an insight into the society that built it. The word 'broch' comes from the Old Norse term for a fortification, *borg*, which implies that many were in reasonable shape in Viking times; Mousa in Shetland was certainly used as a refuge by Norsemen, and there are characteristic Viking Age artefacts from several Orcadian broch-sites.

There has been much argument in academic journals in recent years about what constitutes a broch and how this architectural design developed. The classic definition of a broch is a tall drystone tower, circular and tapering in its diameter as it rises; the upper part of the wall is hollow and there is a single entrance and no windows. The classic example is Mousa in Shetland, which still survives to a height of 13m (43ft). Most other brochs had become very ruinous and it was assumed that originally they spired to the height of Mousa. It is now recognized, however, that Mousa is not typical and that perhaps few were built to such height. Mousa is exceptionally small in diameter with a very thick wall, both features allowing the wall to be built to an unusual height. Current opinion favours a timber and turf roof over the entire broch, supported just below the top of the broch wall, but this would undoubtedly have made the interior very dark; an alternative is that there were roofed timber galleries (there is often evidence for an internal scarcement) and an open central area. As no broch survives to its full height, where there might have been some structural evidence, the question will never be solved one way or the other. Brochs are unique to Scotland, particularly to western and northern Scotland where they must have dominated the contemporary landscape. They conform so closely in overall design that it has been suggested that they were the work of master craftsmen who travelled round undertaking commissions from eminent households who chose to signal their wealth and status by having a broch built. Shown on the map (73) are some 50 brochs known in Orkney, but there are many mounds which could prove on excavation to be brochs, and the true figure is likely to be much higher.

Recent excavations in Orkney have helped to explain how the idea of the broch developed in this area at least, as a stage, perhaps the ultimate stage, in the evolution of the roundhouse. Substantial stone-built roundhouses such as those at Quanterness and Bu are seen to have been the first stage in a process of aggrandisement which led over some 500 years to the fortified tower known to us as the broch. An intermediate stage between simple roundhouse and fully fledged broch was uncovered at Howe, in the form of a two-storey house with a thick wall with two staircases within the wall and a guard cell on either side of the entrance. Built around 300 BC, this house was replaced within 100 or so years by a massive broch tower.

The question of the architectural origin of the broch is, however, complex, and brochs in Orkney cannot be viewed in isolation from those in Shetland and those in mainland and western Scotland. In Shetland, there are forts with massive buildings known as blockhouses which must play a part there in the evolution of the broch. In the Western Isles, there are small stone forts with galleries within the wall, known as galleried duns; these may well have initiated the idea of the hollow wall that could be built to great height.

Brochs have often been likened to the keep of a medieval castle, particularly where there are outer defences enclosing domestic buildings like the bailey of a castle. This is a legitimate, if arguable, comparison of structures, but there is the danger that it implies that similar social systems built them, whereas the feudal system with autocratic chiefs at the top of the hierarchical tree cannot be transposed more than a thousand years to explain brochs. Celtic society had leaders, such as Calgacus who led the tribesmen into battle against Agricola and the Roman army at Mons Graupius. They were not autocrats empowered by the machinery of government but rather leaders who served the corporate wishes of their community.

The distribution of brochs in Orkney is predominantly coastal, and this has led observers to over-emphasize the role of the sea in the way in which brochs functioned. A classic past explanation for brochs has been as look-out posts from which Roman slave-ships might be spotted and in which their hapless targets might find refuge. The fact is that the distribution of most archaeological sites of every type in Orkney is coastal, either because their discovery was the result of coastal erosion or because the coast offered maximum defence possibilities and minimal disruption to good agricultural land. In the case of brochs, a coastal location had many advantages, including defence and marginality to the best land, as well as access to the sea for transport and fishing, but defence appears to have come first for access to the sea was not always immediate or easy. The map shows the

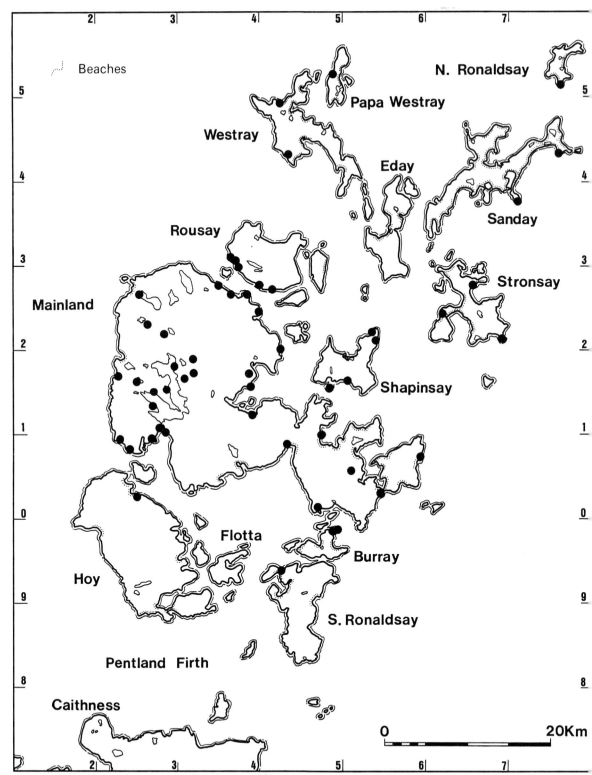

73 *Map of Orkney showing the distribution of confirmed brochs and of beaches.*

distribution of known broch-type structures and of beaches, and the correlation between the two is far from close (see **73**). A map at this scale cannot show the small landing-places suitable for one or two boats, nor can it convey the complex considerations by which a safe anchorage is identified or the factors that can make a landing-place suitable in one set of weather and tide conditions but not in another.

Eynhallow Sound, between mainland and Rousay, is lined with at least eight brochs, which might suggest that it was an important waterway from east to west. But there are tidal problems at the west end of the Sound, which in certain weather conditions make it highly dangerous. With the Atlantic Ocean pushing in from one side and the North Sea pushing in from the other, Orkney is subject to complex tidal interactions; the two tidal systems are out of sequence, with the result that the Atlantic high tide arrives two or three hours before that of the North Sea, and the predominant flow of water is from west to east. Eynhallow Sound is one of several places, including the Pentland Firth, where, when a fast-flowing tidal stream encounters a gale blowing in the opposite direction, roosts or overfalls can occur in the sea which are lethal to small boats. Perhaps the attraction of Eynhallow Sound was its inshore fishing grounds.

Two of the brochs on Eynhallow Sound, Gurness on the mainland coast and Midhowe in the island of Rousay, are not only well-preserved and in the care of the State, but they are also excellent examples of brochs with outer defences and with domestic settlement between the broch and the outer defences (**colour plates 8 and 9**).

Gurness

Most brochs seem to have been built in prominent locations, on cliff-top, promontory or rise. On a calm day the choice of site for the broch at Gurness appears unspectacular, but an easterly gale makes access on foot virtually impossible. The modern visitor has a handy car-park, but previously the headland could be cut off by the

physical problems of getting there. From the top of the broch there would have been a wide view not only over Eynhallow Sound and the islands but also over the Sands of Evie where boats could land and over the fertile hinterland. The rocky shore of the headland has suffered from erosion and it is impossible to judge how much land has been lost, but it seems likely from the surviving shape of the settlement and from the fact that the headland is low-lying that originally the outer defences formed a complete circuit.

The name of the headland is Aiker Ness, and at one time the broch was known by the same name (**74**). The great mound on Aikerness was known to antiquarians as a likely broch-site in the nineteenth century, but interest was rekindled in 1929 by the Orcadian poet, Robert Rendall (p.12). The leg of his painting stool sank into a hole in the top of the mound one day, and he returned with tools and a boy from the farm to help carry out a small exploratory excavation: 'By sheer good luck the first thrust of the spade uncovered what proved to be the top opening of a narrow stone stairway set between solid walls.' The following year full excavation began under

74 *Aerial view of the broch-village at Gurness; the later Pictish houses have been rebuilt in front of the visitor centre, bottom right.*

101

the auspices of the Society of Antiquaries of Scotland, and, after the importance of the site was recognized and it was taken into State guardianship in 1931, the excavation continued until war broke out in 1939. The work of consolidating the structures for public display was resumed after the war, but the excavation was not published. Almost 50 years after the excavation finished, the original notes, plans and artefacts were used by John Hedges to produce after so long an interval an account as close as possible to an excavation report.

The modern route to Gurness is from the west, round the Sands of Evie, but this is to approach the settlement from behind; the entrance-way both through the defences and into the broch is from the east, suggesting that occupants and visitors were more likely to arrive overland than

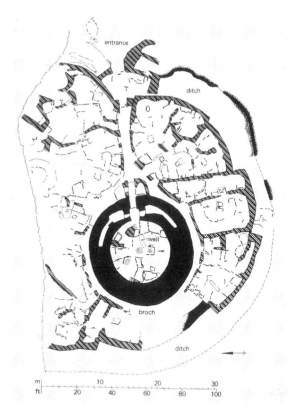

75 (Right) *Plan of the broch and surrounding houses at Gurness.*

76 (Below) *The entrance way leading through the village to the broch at Gurness.*

from the sea via the Sands of Evie. Much has been made of the fact that the entrances into the broch and through the outer defences are on the same alignment, and that a passage-way leads directly from one to the other through the houses outside the broch (**75, 76**). This overall design is thought to prove that all three elements were built at the same time as part of one grand design, but it does no more than indicate that all three elements were interdependent. The building sequence is in fact undocumented. Commonsense suggests that the houses in the space between the broch and the outer defences were built after the broch, but the interval could have been short or long; the design of those close to the broch-entrance suggests that they were built after a 'porch' had been added outside the entrance. The fact that the stepped outer wall of the semi-detached housing units encroaches on the inner ditch of the defences indicates that the latter was already in place and perhaps losing importance when the houses were built (**77**). The outer defences may have been contemporary

with the broch, or, on analogy with the sequence at Howe, they could have belonged to a settlement on the site before the broch was built – the excavation was constrained by the need to preserve standing structures for eventual display to the public, with the result that fugitive traces of earlier occupation would easily remain hidden.

The 'porch' had the effect of masking the entrance, whereas the original design allowed the grandeur of the great lintel over the entrance to be appreciated (**78**). The broch-wall is about 4m (13ft) thick, creating a long passage-way into the interior; about halfway along was the door, which opened inwards. The door itself does not survive, but it may have been of wood or flagstone, and there are bar-holes in the passage walls to accommodate the long wooden beam which locked the door against the checks in the

77 The inner rampart and 'curtain wall' at Gurness.

walls and the sillstone (79). Once the 'porch' was added, the entrance passage became almost 7m (23ft) long and had an outer door, making the approach into the broch an intimidating experience.

Behind the inner door is an opening on either side leading into a guard cell (80) – the bar for the door was operated from within the right-hand cell. These cells also gave access to a ground-level passage and an upper passage within the thickness of the broch wall. Although the broch survives to a height of only about 3.6m (12ft), it was originally considerably higher; traces remain of a ledge on the inner wall which would have supported an upper floor, and part survives of a staircase leading upwards through the wall from an entrance well above the floor of the broch.

Most of the crowded furnishings in the interior were not part of the original design but

78 (Opposite) *The broch-entrance at Gurness.*

79 (Left) *The entrance into the right-hand guard-cell and the hole for the bar that would hold the door closed against the upright stone jamb.*

80 (Right) *Inside a beehive-shaped guard-cell.*

belong to a later occupation. The original fittings certainly included a hearth and a well, but any other features have been masked by later work. As it survives, the circular room, more than 10m (33ft) across, has two hearths and a number of compartments built with upright flagstones, mostly set radially round the wall (81). Beside one of the hearths can still be seen the sockets for vertical posts which supported a spit across the fire.

The buildings outside the broch are a stunning demonstration of what can be achieved with Orkney flagstone. They form a series of semi-detached units consisting of houses and yards, and partitions and cubicles have been created using thin upright flags (82). Each unit has a rectangular hearth, paved and kerbed, in the main living area, and there are cupboards and

81 Inside the broch at Gurness.

82 One of the buildings outside the broch at Gurness, with flagstone partitions and a water-tank beside the hearth.

even a lavatory recognizable by its stone seat.

The excavations at Gurness yielded 850 arte-facts, mostly of stone and bone, and a vast amount of broken pottery from plain barrel-shaped vessels. There were traces of both bronze-working and iron-working in the village, but few bronze objects survived and soil con-ditions led to the destruction of iron through corrosion. Amongst the moulds were some for simple bronze dress-pins and others for knobbed spear-butts, a special type of fitting which was fashionable in Ireland as well as in Scotland. Animal bone, whalebone and antler was used for the long-handled combs which are typical finds from brochs, as well as for needles, socketed handles and mountings. Stone provided a wide variety of equipment, from whetstones for sharpening knives to pivot stones for doors and

quernstones for processing grain. These included not only the old-fashioned saddle quern but also the new and more efficient rotary quern, which was to remain in use into the nineteenth century (83).

In its heyday, Gurness must have been a most impressive sight, from the gatehouse over the rampart and ditch, through the bustling village to the great broch. It was not unique, although it is certainly the best preserved. A very similar establishment was excavated in 1870 at Lingro, overlooking the sandy beach at the head of Scapa Bay to the south of Kirkwall. The neck of land between Scapa Bay and the Bay of Kirkwall is only $1\frac{1}{2}$ miles wide, and there was almost certainly another broch in a similar situation beneath the later streets of Kirkwall. The perimeter of the broch-village at Lingro is a curtain wall as at Gurness, but it is not known whether there was also a ditch and rampart

83 An Orcadian girl grinds corn with a rotary quern in the late nineteenth century.

system; the excavation was never published, although a plan exists and shows no such defences, and the site is now barely visible. The broch and village at Howe lay within substantial defences, and there are doubtless other examples as yet unexcavated. If these villages which could house 200 or more people were planned from the start, along with the broch, they carry implications of fundamental social change. Where were all those people living previously? Not apparently in villages but in individual homes, and their response to the tribal decision to build on a communal scale implies recognition of some new need. It may not be a purely physical coincidence that the most extensive broch-sites are in the least naturally defensive locations, if defence was not the primary consideration. Access to as large as possible an area of agricultural land and grazing may have been paramount.

Midhowe, Rousay

Midhowe is so-called because it is the middle one of a group of three brochs overlooking the west end of Eynhallow Sound; the three are remarkably close together within a stretch of coast that runs from steep cliffs to the north-west to low-lying ground to the south-east. Unfortunately only Midhowe has been excavated and the sequence, if there was a sequence, in the construction and use of the three is unknown. Were they contemporary and should they be seen as a case of pride run riot? Or were they built in chronological sequence and do they represent the needs of a small community over several centuries? They are so close together at the western extremity of the fertile south-west fringe of the island that it seems likely that they belonged to the same unit of land – the same unit that had belonged some two and a half thousand years earlier to the family or clan of the great stalled cairn of Midhowe (pp.50–1) and which, via the eleventh-century Viking estate of Sigurd of Westness, was to become the modern farm of Westness.

The excavation was funded by the landowner, W.G. Grant (p.12), and directed by him and by the Director of the National Museum of Antiquities of Scotland, J.G. Callander, over the four years 1930–3, but the physical work over five summers and a few winter months was an almost single-handed achievement on the part of James K. Yorston, who worked for Grant's Trumland estate in Rousay. It was estimated that he had 'wheeled out from 1500 to 2000 tons of fallen stones and debris'. Meticulous surveys of the structures revealed were the contribution of an excellent draughtsman, David Wilson.

The Broch of Midhowe stands on a low promontory above a rocky shore consisting of the sort of flat-bedded flagstone that was such an ideal source of building stone (84). A geo or inlet cuts into the shore on either side of the promontory, on the south a narrow and very deep geo quite unsuitable for boats and on the north a wider and shallower inlet which could have been used by small boats. The narrow geo is known as Stenchna Geo, stinking geo, on account of the large quantities of rotting seaweed that accumulate there; this handy source of seaweed may have been used to advantage by the people of

84 *Aerial view of the broch at Midhowe.*

Midhowe for fuel and fertiliser. The promontory has clearly been eroded by the sea since broch times, particularly on the north-west where there are the partial remains of a number of buildings outside the broch-tower, but the village is unlikely ever to have been extensive. The outer defences skirt the broch tightly on the landward side, leaving only a metre between them, which suggests that the builders had little choice in terms of space; the same impression of lack of space is given by the secondary buildings tucked in to the angle between the broch wall and the forework.

The landward approach to Midhowe must have been splendidly imposing (85). A massive stone rampart was built in an arc across the promontory between the two geos, widening at one end to form a long entrance passage; except at the entrance, a ditch was dug on either side of the rampart. It seems likely that this rampart was built more for visual effect than for defence, because its southern end stops short of the geo on a natural rock face, leaving below it a ledge along which anyone could walk out to the promontory, bypassing the forework altogether. There are even rock-cut steps leading up from the ledge to the inner end of the entrance passage.

Were the broch and the forework contemporary? This question is unfortunately impossible to answer either from the site stratigraphy or from logic. Given that the source of building stone was the shore, it would have been physically possible to build the broch within an existing fort.

From the passage through the forework, a pathway leads round the broch to its entrance, which, oddly, faces out to sea and into the brunt of the westerly gales. On such a low promontory, the entire settlement must have been drenched frequently in sea-spray. In keeping with the grandeur of the forework, the entrance into the broch is unusually lofty; there is no need here to stoop to enter. The door would have been made of wood and placed into position when needed, but it is difficult here to understand how it was kept in place. There are checks for a door and a sill-stone about half-way down the long entrance passage, but no sign of bar-holes in the wall on either side in which a bar might be inserted to brace the door against the checks. A small corbelled cell opens off either side of the passage on the inner side of the door-checks, and one of them leads into a gallery within the thickness of the broch-wall. Originally this ran round almost the entire base of the broch, but there were evidently structural problems which led to the partial infilling of the passage. The same problems were countered outside the broch by buttressing with upright stones. A sea-wall was built in the 1930s to protect the site from erosion, and the same device of upright stones was used to great effect in creating a strong face against the sea (see 5).

Inside the broch, the wall survives to a maximum height of about 4.3m (14ft), and there is a projecting ledge to support an upper timber floor at a height of about 3.4m (11ft). Below this, but still requiring a ladder to reach it, a doorway opens on to a stair which leads up to an upper gallery and cells within the broch-wall, although these only survive in part. The ground floor is extraordinarily well-furnished and evokes very strongly a sense of domestic life. This is how the broch looked when it was abandoned rather than when it was built; almost nothing is known about the original arrangement of the interior, because, not surprisingly, the excavators were reluctant to destroy the surviving furnishings. There is an underground cellar, cut some 2.6m (8½ft) into the rock, which is likely to have been part of the original design and which appears later to have gone out of use, for its slab cover lies partly beneath a hearth.

The earlier timber mezzanine floor must have been dismantled to allow a total redesign of the interior. This time thin flagstones were used to create partitions, like building with a pack of cards but here the flimsiness is an illusion. The floor space was divided into two separate rooms by a row of upright flags aligned on one side of the entrance passage. When one enters the broch, one can turn left or right, but one cannot pass from one room to the other without

returning to the entrance area. A socket stone on the floor on the left suggests that there was a wooden door to that room. Each room is further subdivided into smaller areas by both high and low upright slabs. In one case, in the north room, great skill has gone into creating an alcove with a corbelled roof balanced on a single tall flag, yet the space enclosed is considerably less than a metre square. A low but carefully dressed hole, large enough for a person to wriggle through, in the flag forming its back wall suggests that the function of the alcove may have been related to access to the next cubicle (despite the fact that it is also possible just to walk round the alcove).

85 Artist's reconstruction of the broch, forework and later buildings phases at the broch of Midhowe, Rousay.

The problem in trying to interpret such structures is twofold. The evidence may be incomplete – a small round hole in the slab forming the inner wall of the alcove suggests that something is missing – and the original design may not have been entirely domestic in purpose. A slab-built cell against the central partition has a hole cut in one slab through which the entrance passage into the broch is visible – or was it simply a means of fastening the door into the room?

There are also hearths and tanks let into the floor in both rooms. They represent a sequence in the life of the broch, for in each room there are two hearths, one partly superimposed on the other; in some cases, the small post-holes are still visible on either side of the hearth in which there would have been uprights to support a spit or rod across the fire. This would be used to roast meat or to suspend cooking pots. The tank in the south room had a carefully fitted stone cover and is fed by a spring of fresh water; the excavators recorded that it retained about 0.3m (1ft) of water which 'remained clear and drinkable all the years the work of excavation was going on'.

A layer of 'peat-like matter' on the floor of the north room suggested that heather and grass had been strewn as a covering. Many domestic tools were found on the floor, including bone pins and points, long-handled bone combs, bone handles and mounts, stone spindle-whorls and loom-weights, whetstones, hammerstones and quern-stones (both saddle and rotary types). Bronze jewellery hints at the wealth and status of the family owning the broch, as do the few imported items of Roman origin such as pottery and a bronze ladle (the latter unfortunately smashed by falling stones). Fragments of crucibles and a mould indicate the activities on the site of a bronzeworker, although the quantity of debris need not represent more than a day's work by an itinerant craftsman.

The remains that survive of buildings outside the broch were certainly not contemporary with the forework, for some were built over the inner ditch and into the inner face of the rampart, and they appear not to have been contemporary with the construction of the broch, although, as always, this point is arguable. They consist of irregular enclosures which probably represent small houses and open yards, and their most interesting features are the cupboards and shelves built into their walls. One was used by a blacksmith, for it contains a substantial hearth which, when excavated, was 'covered with masses of iron slag'. Unfortunately, soil conditions were unsuitable for the preservation of any products made of iron.

Compared to older excavations in which bone other than that made into tools was not considered worth keeping, Midhowe offers considerable insights into the basic economy of the settlement, although no record was published of the quantities of the various species identified. Cattle, sheep and pigs were reared, and red and roe deer were hunted; horse bones were found but nothing is known about the size of the animal. Birds were exploited, including gannets, geese and ducks, and the bones of whales and seals were used, no doubt along with their meat, blubber and skins. Excavation techniques were not such as to enable the recovery of fish-bones, but it is inconceivable that fishing was not part of the economy.

Midhowe is a good example of the problems that surround the interpretation of broch-villages that were excavated before modern techniques of excavation developed and before radiocarbon dating was invented. There are still basic questions that cannot be answered, such as the chronological relationship between the broch and its outer defences and between the broch and the buildings around it, and the date of the whole structural sequence. Even the imported goods of Roman origin, although reasonably well-dated in themselves, cannot be used to date the site closely. Exotic items become heirlooms, and who can say how long or through how many hands an object like the bronze ladle arrived in Rousay. The great grassy mound that covers a ruined broch is a more daunting exercise in excavation now than it was 50 years ago, simply because standards of recording and analysis are higher, involving more people, more time and above all more money. Not surprisingly, only one such mound has been excavated in recent years, Howe near Stromness, and the whole enterprise took almost two decades from lifting the first turf to publication of the results – compared to the five years that Midhowe took from beginning to end.

Beyond the Roman world

Orkney was well beyond the limits of the Roman occupation of Scotland, which effectively ended at the mouths of the Highland glens in Perthshire despite military campaigning which may have reached as far north as the Moray Firth. But the islands were known to the Romans as the *Orcades* and had indeed been known in the classical world since the northern voyage of Pytheas of Marseilles in the 320s BC. This energetic and enquiring Greek explorer sought not only to extend geographical and astronomical knowledge by his voyage but also to obtain much-needed and valued tin and amber. Christopher Hawkes has argued that Pytheas' ship sailed with the Atlantic gulf stream current into the Irish Sea and up the west coast of England and Scotland; in the Outer Isles he learnt of the existence of the land he called Thule, known there because of the migration line of the whooper swan between the Butt of Lewis and Iceland. It was later described as *ultima Thule*, because it was thought to be at the end of the world. Pytheas continued on his voyage via Orkney, and the journey to Thule took five days and five nights from Westray, aided by the long days of summer. On his way back, Pytheas sailed via Shetland into the Baltic for his amber before returning to the northern tip of Scotland and thence sailing southwards in order to complete a circumnavigation of Britain.

The identity of Thule became, and has remained, contentious, but the existence of Orkney was recognized. When Britain was invaded by the Roman army under the Emperor Claudius in AD 43, he and his generals had a reasonable idea of its geography. Writing some 300 years later, Eutropius claimed that the islands of Orkney submitted to Claudius, implying that Orcadian leaders were in southern England to do so. Until recently, the tendency has been to discount Eutropius' report as an exaggeration, but an engaging interpretation of archaeological evidence by Andrew Fitzpatrick suggests that there may be some truth at least in a link between Orkney and the south of England. Two unusual sherds of pottery were found at the broch of Gurness, identified as part of a distinctive type of amphora or wine jar imported from the continent where they were made during the period from about 20 BC to about AD 60. The Gurness example is more than 600 miles north of other examples which are mostly in south-east England. Unfortunately the exact find-spots of the two sherds from Gurness are not known, only that one came from the broch itself and one from the outbuildings, which means that it is impossible to be certain that the amphora reached Orkney within the period of manufacture of this class of pottery. Nevertheless, there remains the intriguing possibility that this exotic import supports the idea of a direct link between Orkney and southern England, if not the notion that there were Orcadian chieftains in attendance upon Claudius. If the amphora arrived intact, it is likely to have held either olives preserved in a liqueur wine or the wine on its own – an unexpected addition to the Orcadian diet!

It is nevertheless unlikely that any lasting formal relationship was established between Rome and Orkney, given the remoteness of the islands from the arena of Roman operations in Britain. After the battle of Mons Graupius in AD 83, the Roman General Agricola 'ordered his admiral to coast round Britain', presumably northwards from the east coast of Scotland;

Tacitus relates that the fleet was 'sped by favouring winds and fame'. This was partly a fact-finding exercise to confirm that Britain was indeed an island and partly a triumphal progress which warned of 'the terror of Rome'.

Sherds of other types of Roman pottery have been found on several broch sites, including the fine red tableware known as samian ware; this and a few coins suggest that Roman goods were beginning to reach the far north of Scotland in the second century AD, several decades after the invasion of Scotland under Agricola in AD 79. The volume of goods was never high, though the trickle was maintained into the fourth century. A beautiful glass cup of fourth-century date was buried in a cist in Westray, and other glassware, once broken, is likely to have been melted down and reused to make the bangles that were popular. Perhaps even more telling than the imports themselves are the objects made locally in imitation of Roman goods, for these reflect a strong desire to emulate the Roman life-style. Finds from the broch of Oxtrow in Birsay included a sandstone lamp carved in the shape of a Roman pottery lamp, and Gurness yielded a copy of a bronze ladle like that from Midhowe but made in steatite. The steatite itself was imported, probably from Shetland where the nearest outcrops of this relatively soft stone are found.

The wealth that lay behind the acquisition of prestigious goods, whether they arrived by barter or as marriage or diplomatic gifts, was based on land and livestock – cattle, sheep and horses. Successful breeding provided not just for the day-to-day sustenance and transport for the household but live animals which could be translated into marketable goods and which conveyed to others the visible wealth and standing of their owners. They could be given in payment or in recompense or to impress. Their products, such as skins and dried meat, needed to be stored in a cool place, as did seed-corn and any surplus grain, with the result that underground cellars became a regular feature of wealthy households.

Cellars and wells

The broch at Midhowe was furnished with both a well and a cellar, although the well is unexpectedly shallow compared to the cellar, and it may be that underground structures in other brochs were cellars rather than wells as is usually assumed. Most have steps leading down to an underground chamber, yet steps are unnecessary in a well, where lowering a bucket on a rope will do the job quite adequately. The broch at Burroughston in Shapinsay has such a well (no longer visible), a simple shaft, 3m (10ft) deep, with direct access from the floor of the broch. In contrast, the 'well' in the broch of Netlater in mainland Orkney was found on excavation in the nineteenth century to have a passage which led underground to a flight of steps and thence to a 'cistern', and the mainland broch known as the Knowe of Burrian had a short passage leading to steep stairs and a double, figure-of-eight-shaped chamber. In neither case was there enough water or even dampness to suggest access to a spring, although it is possible that the level of the water-table has changed over the intervening 2000 years. In some cases, where there are side-chambers and recesses together with a water source, they may have been designed to perform both as wells and storage cellars.

The best and most elaborate example of a well-cum-cellar is in the broch of Gurness and it is still accessible (86). Beneath a flagstone is a flight of stairs leading down to a ledge in the well-chamber, the floor of which is about 4.5m (15ft) below the broch floor and which is fed by a spring. The water is now only about 0.35m (1ft) deep, and a depth greater than a metre would have flooded the ledge, yet the well-chamber has a corbelled and lintelled roof at a height of 4m (13ft). Above that, and accessible from the stair, are two small storage chambers, and a hidden entrance in the stair leads to two larger chambers. One of these is 2.5m (8ft) high and barely 0.5m (1ft 7in) wide – large enough for one person standing. Is this a prison like the pit-prisons of medieval castles? Or a secret place from which an 'oracle' might speak, heard but unseen? This is clearly more than a well, and it may have been more than a cellar for storage. There were strong water-cults among the Celts, and wells were often endowed with supernatural powers; though an artificial well, the Gurness example was supplied by a natural spring and its manipulation may have increased the prestige of its owner. Its construction was certainly an impressive achievement, which began with quarrying into the bedrock to create a hole some 5m across and 4.5m deep (17 by 15ft), within which the chambers and stair were built. It seems logical that most if not all of this work would have been completed before the broch was built.

Earth-houses

Underground cellars existed independent of brochs. In Orkney they are known as earth-houses, but they are not confined to the islands and in mainland Scotland are also known as weems or by the French term *souterrain*. They are also found in Ireland, Cornwall and Brittany, but their design and date vary as widely as their distribution and, in Scotland at least, they are best regarded as a common solution to storage needs. The Orkney examples form a discrete group, however, which is likely to reflect a custom popular from about 600 BC into the early centuries AD. They consist essentially of a passage and an oval chamber, and, unlike the earth-houses of Perthshire and Angus, the roofs of which were visible at ground level, the Orcadian examples were entirely underground. They are usually discovered when they collapse under the weight of a tractor!

Some 25 earth-houses have been recorded in Orkney, mostly in mainland but with examples in Hoy and Eday. There were undoubtedly more, some unrecorded and others yet to be found. Only three have been excavated in recent years, and most of the available information comes from discoveries made many years ago – an example at Grain on the outskirts of Kirkwall

86 *A stone stair leads down into the well at Gurness.*

was one of the earliest monuments in Orkney to be taken into State care. It had first been discovered in about 1827 but was closed up until 1857 when Farrer and Petrie decided to explore it. Its state of preservation was so good that it was taken into guardianship in 1908 as an excellent example of a typical Orcadian earth-house. Unfortunately no good record was made of the 'excavation', but it is clear that the chamber was empty and that the old land surface above it bore extensive traces of domestic settlement; there were 'walls running in various directions' and 'a large pit' full of midden material. The 'large pit' may have been part of another earth-house, for, during an excavation in 1982 of a small area adjacent to the existing earth-house, parts of another two earth-houses were found, again along with traces of surface settlement. One earth-house appeared to replace the other in sequence, but it was not possible to excavate them entirely. The earth-house found last century is one of the deepest known, reaching a depth of 3.7m (12ft) in the chamber with some 2m (6½ft) of soil above the roof, but depth appears to be related to geology; here the builders dug down until they reached bedrock, which gave them a solid and dry floor. Elsewhere in Orkney the bedrock was higher or the earth-house was dug into solid clay, and in clay situations it was apparently not considered necessary to line the sides with walling. Two earth-houses, at Howe near Stromness and Rowiegar in Rousay, were economically constructed within defunct chambered tombs.

Because of its depth, steps were needed at Grain in order to reach the passage, but elsewhere a hatch gave direct access into the passage. As at Grain (87), the passage often curves round

and into the chamber, and it is usually possible to stand almost upright in the chamber whereas the approach along the passage may involve crouching. Typically, the roof of the passage consists of horizontal slabs and the chamber is roofed with a combination of corbelling and lintels supported on stone pillars (88). Despite their apparent isolation, which is simply the result of poor recording in the past, these earth-houses were part of ground-level domestic settlements, for which they acted as cellars (89). Several accounts of old discoveries mention kitchen midden filling the entrance to the earth-house, and modern excavations have found midden fillings, while at Howe there was evidence of the contemporary

87 *Entrance passage into the earth-house at Grain; the floor was lowered by cutting into the bedrock in modern times to make access easier.*

88 *Inside the earth-house at Rennibister.*

roundhouse. The reconstruction drawing is based on the earth-house at Rennibister in mainland Orkney, which was discovered in 1926 when its roof gave way beneath the weight of a threshing machine; although there was no excavation at ground-level to seek the contemporary house, there is likely to have been a stone-walled roundhouse from which entry to the earth-house could be gained via a slab-covered hatch in the floor. Rennibister lies beneath the yard of the modern farm, a neat example of the re-use over the centuries of a good location.

An odd aspect of Rennibister is the discovery of disarticulated human remains on the floor of the chamber. The bones represent six adults, male and female, and twelve children of various ages, perhaps three or four families. There were no artefacts to give any clue as to the date of the bones, and, because they were thoroughly mixed together, they must have been placed in the earth-house as bones rather than as bodies – but when? and why?

Towards history

Names play a vital role in human society. Personal names, family names, place-names, these are all essential to our understanding and manipulation of the world we inhabit. An enormous limitation to the reconstruction of the past offered by prehistoric archaeology is that this element is missing and that the people are correspondingly remote. Not one Orcadian can be named until medieval times. The name Orkney preserves an early Celtic tribal name,

Orc; this means 'the young pigs' and is thought perhaps to reflect a traditional totem, but it is impossible to estimate how long the people of the islands were so named and when it became no more than a place-name.

By the sixth century AD, Orkney was part of Pictland and shared the material culture of the Picts, including symbol stones, as well as their social organization. The single most influential development in Orkney in Pictish times was the introduction of Christianity. Conversion was doubtless a gradual process, beginning perhaps in the sixth century with a few missionary monks and reaching full fruition in the

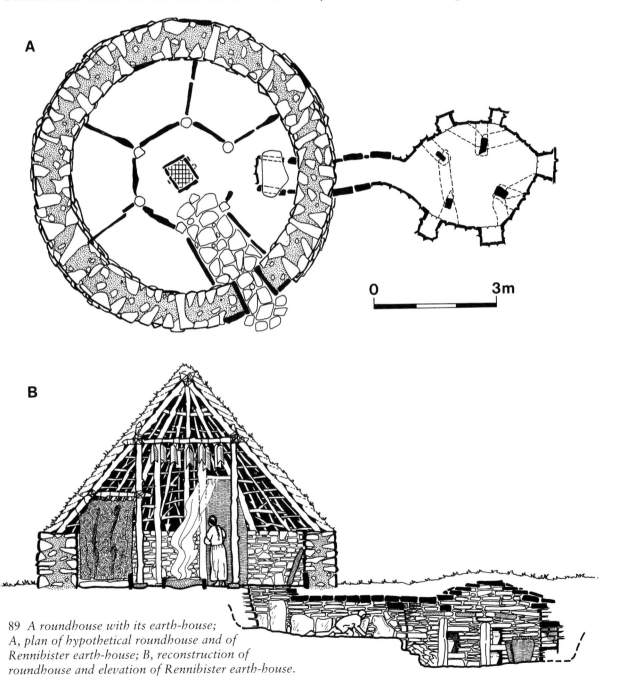

89 *A roundhouse with its earth-house;*
A, plan of hypothetical roundhouse and of
Rennibister earth-house; B, reconstruction of
roundhouse and elevation of Rennibister earth-house.

117

90 *Artist's reconstruction of the early Christian altar from Flotta.*

eighth. Christianity brought literacy and the artistic accomplishments of the early medieval world, though there are few physical traces in the archaeological record apart from sculpture and church furniture such as hand-bells.

The island of Flotta is best known today for its oil terminal, but it has a much earlier claim to fame. This small island between Hoy and South Ronaldsay had its own church in the eighth century, and inside the church was a beautifully carved stone altar (90); all that survives is the front panel, now in the National Museums of Scotland as one of the finest and earliest pieces of church furniture.

By the eighth century, the Christian Church was well established in Orkney, and there is evidence to suggest that there may have been a resident bishop, probably with his seat in Papa Westray, and that this organized ecclesiastical structure survived the process of raiding and settlement by the Vikings in the late eighth and ninth centuries. As it entered the Viking Age, Orkney found itself centre stage. After 5000 years of playing a supporting role on the fringe of the British Isles, Orkney became the focus of a new world set in the North Atlantic.

CHAPTER EIGHT

Monumental folklore

'The Orkney imagination is haunted by time.' George Mackay Brown wrote of the islands and people in a book, *The Orkney Tapestry*, that was published in 1969, and his words evoke the sense of the past that is hard to avoid in Orkney. Native Orcadians seem to be born with it, and newcomers soon acquire it. A consciousness of the past is essential to the future, as Edmund Burke recognized in the eighteenth century: 'People will not look forward to posterity who never look back to their ancestors.' Perhaps it is easier to be aware of the past in a place as littered with ancestral debris as Orkney.

Sir Walter Scott visited the Northern Isles in 1814, and he was much taken with the antiquities, weaving many into his story, *The Pirate*, which is set in Orkney and Shetland. The climax of the tale takes place at the Stones of Stenness, which he describes as 'the phantom forms of antediluvian giants', while at the same time contriving to provide an antiquarian account of their height and disposition and of the current theories about their original use. Scott's imagined altar-table became reality when the site was reconstructed in 1907 (**91**).

Many prehistoric monuments were such obvious features of the Orcadian landscape that they must have become part of local folklore from an early period – earlier, probably, than the Viking Age. Huge mounds and standing stones and man-made (or troll-made?) holes in the ground were part of the very fabric of Orkney. Odin's Stone, near the Stones of Stenness, was a standing stone with a natural hole through it, and it was held in particularly high regard for its magical properties (**92**). Young people came from every part of the islands to seal their love by clasping hands through the hole, and crippled arms and legs were thrust through the hole in the belief that they might be healed. This trust in the power of the stone led to the public uproar that resulted from its destruction in 1814 (p.11).

Other standing stones were regarded either as supernatural missiles or as petrified giants – George Mackay Brown's 'sun-stricken giants'. In the island of Sanday, there is an enormous natural boulder at Scar, which, according to local tradition, had been flung from Eday by a witch whose daughter had eloped with her lover to Sanday. The Stane o' Quoybune at Birsay (**93**) was thought to be a petrified giant, who came to life at the start of every New Year's Day; the stone was thought to go down to the Loch of Boardhouse for a drink, but it had to be back in its place before dawn. Heaven help any mortal who witnessed this happening – he or she would not live to celebrate another new year.

In the island of Hoy is an extraordinary rock-cut chamber which is thought probably to have been a Neolithic tomb. The great block of sandstone, into which the chamber has been cut, lies in a most inhospitable valley at the south-east foot of Ward Hill, the highest hill in Orkney (**94**). There is no direct dating evidence for the monument, other than that it was already in existence when one H. Ross carved his name in

1735, but the design of the interior appears to be related to simple chambered tombs. This natural block of stone is about 8.6m (28ft) long, 4m (13ft) wide and some 2m (6½ft) thick, and into it has been cut a short passage with a small cell on either side. In front of the entrance lies a large stone, which was observed in the sixteenth century to be sealing the entrance to the passage. The most extraordinary of the several inscriptions cut into the rock-surface of the tomb in recent centuries is one cut in 1850 spelling the name of Major W. Mounsey backwards in Latin, and below a line of Persian calligraphy that reads 'I have sat two nights and so learnt patience' (95). Major Mounsey was a former British spy in Afganistan and Persia, who camped at the Dwarfie Stane and endured the midges for two nights.

The dwarf in folklore was a special craftsman. The two aspects of Hoy that seem to have been important in Neolithic times were its pronounced profile seen from afar and the veins of haematite at its north end. Is it possible that these magical attributes were acknowledged by contemporary peoples by the furnishing of a unique form of tomb for a special class of craftsman whose task it was to mine the haematite and to maintain a dialogue with the gods?

Almost every mound had its legendary inhabitant known as 'hogboy' or 'hogboon', after the Old Norse words for 'mound-dweller'. The hogboy was a rather bad-tempered character who was credited with great strength, and he seems to have been a Viking import. The burial-mounds of founders of farms in Norway were held in great respect, and their inhabitants were regarded as guardian spirits for the well-being of the farm. This idea took root in Orkney. Norna, in *The Pirate*, 'learned to visit each lonely barrow – each lofty cairn – to tell its appropriate

93 *The Stane O'Quoybune in Birsay.*

tale, and to soothe with rhymes in his praise the spirit of the stern warror who dwelt within'.

Folklore enriches our perception of the past by trying to explain with words and names and stories the enigmatic elements in the landscape. Prehistoric archaeology attempts to reconstruct the lifestyles of people who must remain nameless but whose material achievements still survive after thousands of years. Orkney is fortunate in its rich archaeological inheritance, and work in years to come will open even wider this unique window into the remote past.

91 (Top left) *The Stones of Stenness in 1907 with the newly erected 'altar'.*

92 (Bottom left) *Odin's Stone, which once stood near the Stones of Stenness.*

94 *The Dwarfie Stane in Hoy, a rock-cut tomb.*

95 *The Dwarfie Stane: a nineteenth-century visitor carved inscriptions both in Persian and in Latin.*

Monuments and museums to visit

Sites in the care of Historic Scotland are open to the public, but those not in State care or open to the public through other bodies lie on privately owned land, and permission to visit must be sought from the landowner. There are several guidebooks with details of monuments and how to find them, which are listed under **Further reading**, including Historic Scotland's official guide to sites in State care, *The Ancient Monuments of Orkney*. Many artefacts from Orkney are in the collections of the National Museums of Scotland in Edinburgh.

Mainland Orkney

Broch of Borwick (NGR HY 224167)
Broch in dramatic location on the west coast; the entrance and landward half of the broch are well preserved (privately owned).

Barnhouse (NGR HY 307127)
Partially reconstructed Neolithic settlement (see pp.38–9) (Orkney Islands Council).

Barnhouse Stone (NGR HY 312121)
Standing stone (privately owned, but visible from the road).

Brough of Birsay (NGR HY 239285)
Pictish well and cast of symbol stone, also Norse houses, church and monastery; this is a tidal island and access depends upon low tide (Historic Scotland).

Cuween (NGR HY 364127)
Chambered cairn (see p.48) (Historic Scotland).

Grain (NGR HY 441116)
Earth-house (see p.114) (Historic Scotland).

Gurness (NGR HY 381268)
Broch and settlement, visitor centre (see pp.101–8) (Historic Scotland).

Maes Howe (NGR HY 318127)
Chambered tomb (see pp.55–9) (Historic Scotland).

Rennibister (NGR HY 397125)
Earth-house (see pp.116–17) (Historic Scotland).

Ring of Brodgar (NGR HY 294133)
Henge and stone circle (see pp.78–9) (Historic Scotland).

Skara Brae (NGR HY 231187)
Neolithic settlement (see pp.28–37) (Historic Scotland).

Stane o'Quoybune, Birsay (NGR HY 253263)
Standing stone (see p.119) (privately owned, but visible from the road).

Stones of Stenness and Watch Stone (NGR HY 306125)
Henge and stone circle and standing stone (see pp.74–8, 81–2) (Historic Scotland).

Stromness Museum, Alfred Street, Stromness
Displays include geology and natural history and some prehistoric artefacts.

Tankerness House Museum, Broad Street, Kirkwall
Excellent displays about early settlers, broch-builders, Picts and Vikings.

Unstan (NGR HY 282117)
Chambered cairn (see pp.51–4) (Historic Scotland)

Wideford (NGR HY 409121)
Chambered cairn (see pp.48–9) (Historic Scotland).

Eday

Stone of Setter (NGR HY 564371)
Standing stone (privately owned, but visible from the road).

Vinquoy (NGR HY 560381)
Chambered cairn (see p.48) (Orkney Islands Council).

Hoy

Dwarfie Stane (NGR HY 243004)
Rock-cut chambered tomb (see pp.61, 119, 121–2) (Historic Scotland).

Papa Westray

Backiskaill (NGR HY 485509)
Crescentic burnt mound (see p.94) (privately owned).

Holm of Papa Westray North (NGR HY 504522)
Chambered cairn (see pp.41–4) (privately owned)

Holm of Papa Westray South (NGR HY 509518)
Chambered cairn (see pp.41, 51) (Historic Scotland).

Knap of Howar (NGR HY 483518)
Neolithic settlement (see pp.23–8) (Historic Scotland).

Rousay

Blackhammer (NGR HY 414276)
Chambered cairn (see p.44) (Historic Scotland).

Knowe of Yarso (NGR HY 404279)
Chambered cairn (see pp.50, 64) (Historic Scotland).

Midhowe (NGR HY 371306)
Broch (see pp.108–12) (Historic Scotland).

Midhowe (NGR HY 372304)
Chambered cairn (see pp.50–1) (Historic Scotland).

Taversoe Tuick (NGR HY 425276)
Two-storey chambered cairn (see pp.47–8) (Historic Scotland).

Sanday

Quoyness (NGR HY 676377)
Chambered cairn (see p.60) (Historic Scotland)

South Ronaldsay

Castle of Burwick (NGR HD 434842)
Promontory fort (privately owned).

Isbister (NGR HD 470845)
Chambered cairn (see pp.54–5) (privately owned, but open to the public on request).

Liddle (NGR HD 464841)
Excavated burnt mound (see p.94) (privately owned, but open to the public on request).

Further reading

Armit, Ian (ed.) *Beyond the Brochs: changing perspectives on the Atlantic Scottish Iron Age*, Edinburgh University Press, Edinburgh, 1990

Bell, Martin and Walker, M.J.C. *Late Quaternary Environmental Change*, Longman, London, 1992

Berry, R.J. and Firth, H.N. (eds) *The People of Orkney*, The Orkney Press, Kirkwall, 1986

Brown, George Mackay *An Orkney Tapestry*, Gollancz, London, 1969

Brown, George Mackay *Portrait of Orkney*, John Murray, London, 1981

Burl, Aubrey *The Stone Circles of the British Isles*, London, 1976

Burl, Aubrey *Prehistoric Astronomy and Ritual*, Shire Archaeology, Princes Risborough, 1983

Clarke, D.V., Cowie, T.G. and Foxon, A *Symbols of Power at the time of Stonehenge*, Edinburgh, 1985

Clarke, David and Maguire, Patrick *Skara Brae: northern Europe's best preserved prehistoric village*, Historic Scotland, Edinburgh, 1989

Davidson, J.L. and Henshall, A.S. *The Chambered Cairns of Orkney*, Edinburgh University Press, Edinburgh, 1989

Dickson, Neil *An Island Shore: the life and work of Robert Rendall*, The Orkney Press, Kirkwall, 1990

Hedges, John *The Tomb of the Eagles*, John Murray, London, 1984

Hedges, John Bu, *Gurness and the Brochs of Orkney, British Archaeological Reports*, nos 163–5, Oxford, 1987

MacKie, Euan *Science and Society in Prehistoric Britain*, Elek, London, 1977

Marwick, Ernest W. *The Folklore of Orkney and Shetland*, Batsford, London, 1975

Miller, Ronald *Orkney*, Batsford, London, 1976

Renfrew, Colin *Investigations in Orkney*, Thames and Hudson, London, 1979

Renfrew, Colin (ed.) *The Prehistory of Orkney BC 4000–1000 AD*, Edinburgh University Press, Edinburgh, 1985

Ritchie, Anna *Orkney and Shetland*, HMSO, Edinburgh, 1985

Ritchie, Anna *Scotland BC*, HMSO, Edinburgh, 1988

Ritchie, Anna *Picts*, HMSO, Edinburgh, 1989

Ritchie, Anna and Breeze, David *Invaders of Scotland*, HMSO, Edinburgh, 1991

Ritchie, Anna and Ritchie, J.N.G. *The Ancient Monuments of Orkney*, HMSO, Edinburgh, 1978

Ritchie, Graham and Ritchie, Anna *Scotland: archaeology and early history*, Edinburgh University Press, Edinburgh, 1991

Ritchie, Graham *Brochs of Scotland*, Shire Archaeology, Princes Risborough, 1988

Thom, A. *Megalithic Lunar Observatories*, Clarendon Press, Oxford, 1971

Thomson, William P.L. *History of Orkney*, Mercat Press, Edinburgh, 1987

Wickham-Jones, Caroline *Scotland's First Settlers*, Batsford, London, 1994

Glossary

backfilling The deliberate filling in of a pit or trench.

barrow An earthen mound raised over burials.

cairn A mound of stones.

check A step, or narrowing, in the walls of an entrance against which a door can be closed.

cist A pit lined and often covered with stone slabs; used for storage or for burials.

corbelled Courses of horizontal stones placed overlapping one another.

cordon A strip of clay applied before firing to the surface of a pot as decoration.

disarticulated skeleton The bones are jumbled together, rather than in their correct anatomical positions.

drystone Built with stones but without mortar.

geo A narrow inlet of the sea, or cleft in the cliffs.

jamb The side-slab of a doorway.

lintel A horizontal stone placed over an entrance.

midden A domestic rubbish heap.

pellet A small ball of clay applied before firing to the surface of a pot as decoration.

quern A stone tool for grinding corn.

rotary quern A quern consisting of two circular stones, the upper of which can be turned by a handle.

saddle quern A quern consisting of a dished or saddle-shaped stone in which corn can be crushed with a smaller hand-held stone.

skerry An isolated rock, often covered by the sea at high water.

spindle-whorl A circular weight, usually made of stone, with a central perforation to take the wooden spindle; used to spin fibres into thread.

steatite A soft stone or talc, also known as soapstone, which is easy to carve.

tang The extension of a stone or metal tool by which it can be fastened to a handle.

temper Stone grit or crushed shell added to clay to strengthen pottery.

whetstone A hard fine-grained stone on which metal blades can be sharpened by friction.

Index